making beautiful bead & wire jewelry

making beautiful
bead & wire jewelry

30 *step-by step projects from materials old and new*

LINDA JONES

CICO BOOKS
LONDON NEW YORK

dedication

This book is dedicated to my beautiful mother and best friend
on her 80th year, who has always nurtured and encouraged
my creativity and helped me to believe I can attain my dreams.

Published in 2010 by CICO Books
An imprint of Ryland Peters & Small Ltd

20–21 Jockey's Fields   519 Broadway, 5th Floor
London WC1R 4BW   New York, NY 10012

www.cicobooks.com

10 9 8 7 6 5 4

Text © Linda Jones 2010
Design and photography © CICO Books 2010

A CIP catalog record for this book is available from the Library of Congress
and the British Library.

ISBN: 978 1 907030 66 6

Printed in China

Editor: Sarah Hoggett
Designer: David Fordham
Photographers: Geoff Dann (steps); David Munns, Stuart West
Stylist: Luis Peral-Aranda

 For digital editions, visit
www.cicobooks.com/apps.php

contents

introduction

In the ten years or so that I've been making bead and wire jewelry, one of the biggest thrills for me has been seeing more and more people discover the pleasure of making unique, one-off pieces of costume jewelry for themselves. However, in these recession-hit times, we're all looking for ways to save money—so my aim in this book is to show you how you can create pieces of designer jewelry for next to nothing. Here are my top money-saving tips.

Bead stores, as anyone who's ever visited one will know, are extremely seductive places and it's easy to get carried away and buy things you don't really need and can't afford. Look out for special offers and wholesale beads online to avoid making expensive impulse purchases. Set a limit on the amount you want to spend and make sure you stick to it—and don't forget to include the cost of postage and packaging to your total.

If you already have some expensive focal beads, or come across some that you simply can't resist buying, use them just at the front of a necklace, not all the way around. The sides and back can be ribbon, cord, chain, or even nylon filament, as in the Vintage Button Necklace on page 95.

Recycle! Tell all your friends and family that you are making jewelry and would welcome any broken, or old, pieces that they might be thinking of getting rid of. Broken chains can be cut up and suspended into chained tassels; and necklaces and bracelets can be taken apart and reassembled into new designs. Even a lone earring can be transformed into a pendant. Thrift stores, flea markets, and garage sales are all great sources of inexpensive jewelry components, too, and you can often find second-hand pieces at knock-down prices that you can take apart and make into a number of stunning new creations.

Last, but most important of all, be inventive and improvise with objects around you. Discarded electrical cable has a wealth of copper wire within it, while florist's wire and even gardening wire can form the basis for a piece of jewelry. Look in your household tool box and sewing box for components: humble washers and bolts make graphic, contemporary-looking "beads," as do old buttons. Interestingly-shaped pebbles and colorful shells can be wrapped with wire to become focal points in a design, and pretty feathers picked up on a country walk can add a flamboyant finishing touch to a brooch or hair accessory. Combining everyday objects with traditional beads in this way not only brings down the cost, but also enables you to produce unique pieces of wearable art!

In designing the projects for this book, I've had great fun thinking laterally and trying to find new uses for things that are not traditional jewelry components. Whether you're an experienced jeweler or completely new to this craft, I hope this book will open your mind, strengthen your wire-working skills, and spark your imagination with renewed creativity.

LINDA JONES

tools

One of the joys of making wire and beaded jewelry is that you require very little in the way of specialty tools and equipment—and everything you need is readily available from craft suppliers, mail-order catalogs, and, of course, the Internet at very affordable prices. Here are my suggestions for a basic tool kit.

HAMMER AND FLAT STEEL STAKE

These tools are used to flatten and toughen wire motifs (see page 20). Specialty jewelry hammers are generally smaller and lighter than general-purpose household hammers, but you can use any hammer as long as one end has a flat, smooth, polished surface. Steel stakes can be bought from specialty jewelry stores, but any flat steel surface will do provided surface has no bumps or abrasions—otherwise the wire will pick up any irregularities that are present.

PLIERS

From top to bottom: Round-, flat-, and chain-nose pliers. Round-nose pliers have round, tapered shafts; they are used to coil and bend wire into small loops and curves and to make jump rings. Chain-nose and flat-nose pliers are both used to grip the wire firmly as you work and to bend it at right angles and angular shapes. However, chain-nose pliers are tapered and narrow and therefore are extremely useful when working on intricate, more delicate pieces. They are also essential for neatening ends.

RING MANDREL OR TRIBLET

Available from specialty jewelry stores, a mandrel is used to form circular shapes such as rings and bangles. Alternatively, shape your wire around any cylindrical object of the appropriate size.

WIRE CUTTERS

Several kinds of wire cutter are available, but I find that "side cutters" are the most useful as they have small, tapered blades that can cut into small spaces. Remember to hold the cutters perpendicular to the wire when cutting to achieve a clean, flush cut.

JIG AND PEGS

A jig consists of a base board with evenly spaced holes and moveable pegs with tops of different diameters, which you arrange in a pattern. You then wrap wire around the pegs to create a wire design. Some jig grids are based on a square and some on the diagonal, so you may have to alter the project patterns slightly to suit your make of jig.

materials

Wire, ribbon, chain, and cord are all essential jewelry-making materials. Wire can be manipulated into all kinds of shapes, while beads, charms, and other items can be suspended from ribbon, chain, and cord.

WIRE

Colored wires are usually copper based with enamel coatings; they must not be over-manipulated as this can remove the surface color. Gold- or silver-plated wires are far less expensive than precious-metal wires and will not tarnish so quickly. All wires come in different thicknesses or "gauges." The lower the gauge number, the thicker the wire—so 18-gauge wire is thicker than 26-gauge wire.

WHICH WIRE TO USE

26-gauge (0.4mm)	Binding, knitting, and weaving
24-gauge (0.6mm)	Threading small delicate beads, binding, and twisting
20-gauge (0.8mm)	General-purpose jewelry work
18-gauge (1mm)	Chunky pieces, framing, and ring shanks
12-gauge (2mm)	Bold, chunky jewelry

CHAIN

Home improvements stores stock a wide range of chains mainly for use in plumbing—an inexpensive alternative to specialty jewelry chains. However, you will also find a fantastic array of shapes, styles, and types in bead stores, from color-coated aluminum to silver- and gold-plated.

RIBBON

If you want to hang a pendant, ribbon provides a softer-looking, more delicate, alternative to wire or chain. From silky satin ribbon to plush velvet, there is a vast choice of widths, colors, patterns, and textures.

CORD

Leather, suede, and cotton cord comes in different widths and colors and is suitable for more informal-looking pieces of jewelry such as lariats and simple bead chokers. You can also use shoe and bootlaces if you've got nothing else to hand.

beads, bolts, and buttons

Specialty bead stores contain literally thousands of different sizes and types, arranged by both color and size. However, one of the intentions of this book is to encourage you to use materials that you might not immediately associate with jewelry. Inexpensive buttons, everyday household items such as washers and bolts, pebbles and shells that you pick up on the beach or on a country walk—once you learn to see them with a creative eye, all can be incorporated into unique, one-off pieces.

LAMPWORK AND FOIL-LINED GLASS BEADS
Look out for foil-lined beads, which provide extra luminosity, and handmade glass to add originality to your pieces.

PEARL BEADS
You can purchase "pearl" beads in varying sizes and colors. The less expensive types are plastic based; glass coated "pearls" have a better luster and glow.

FACETED GLASS CRYSTALS
In addition to the famous Swarovski brand of crystal, you can purchase faceted beads in glass as well as plastic. Various shapes and sizes are available, from round to bicone and teardrop.

METAL BEADS
Metal and metal-coated plastic beads are readily available in all shapes and sizes and are useful as spacers as well as focal beads.

WOOD AND BONE BEADS
You can create stylish, yet casual, jewelry pieces using hand-carved wood and bone beads strung on natural materials such as leather and suede.

FEATURE GLASS BEADS
Collect striking glass beads from old, broken jewelry pieces to provide inspiration for a new design. Study one bead and use the colors and shape as a starting point and construct your whole design around it.

GLASS NUGGETS AND SEED BEADS
Glass nuggets (known colloquially to some people as "dragons' droppings"!) make inexpensive, yet sparkly-looking centerpieces, while tiny seed beads add all-important splashes of color to delicate designs. The size of a seed bead refers to the number that will fit into 1 in. (2.5 cm) when laid end to end—so the higher the number, the smaller the bead.

FINDINGS

Findings is the term used to describe ready-made components such as chains, ear wires, clasps, jump rings, brooch backs, and so on. These can be bought from craft and hobby stores; alternatively, you can create your own by following the step-by-steps in the techniques section (pages 16–21). Ready-made findings come in a variety of colors and metal finishes.

SEMI-PRECIOUS CHIP STONES

Semi-precious chip stones are sold in 16- or 18-in. (40- or 45-cm) lengths. Always buy them ready threaded, so that you know they are fully drilled. When you are ready to use them, snip the thread that holds them together and store them in small containers.

BUTTONS

Incorporated into beaded designs, buttons can add weight, splashes of color, and a sense of fun to your jewelry. Ask to look in your grandmother's sewing box or unpick them from a worn-out garment.

FOUND ITEMS

Pebbles, shells, and feathers are wonderful additions to unique jewelry designs, especially when incorporated into hair accessories and brooches. Keep your eyes open when you are walking in the countryside or along a beach and start a collection for future projects.

WASHERS AND BOLTS

Steel and rubber washers and bolts are available in every hardware store and can give your jewelry designs a contemporary look.

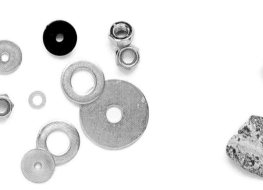

basic techniques

Threading beads and making a link

The basic principle is to construct a neat circle of wire (known as a "link") at each end of the bead, which is then used to suspend the bead from a chain or to connect one bead to another.

1 Working from the spool, thread your chosen bead onto the wire, leaving about ½ in. (1 cm) of wire extending on each side.

2 Remove the bead and cut the wire with your wire cutters.

When you've threaded the bead, hold each link firmly in the jaws of your pliers and twist until both links face the same way—otherwise they will twist around when linked together as a chain.

3 Thread the bead back onto the cut wire. Holding the wire vertically, with the bead in the center, use the tips of your round-nose pliers to bend the wire at a right angle, at the point where it touches the bead.

4 Hold and squeeze the very end of the bent wire tightly with your round-nose pliers and curl it round to form a small circle, following the contour of your pliers. It is better to do this in several short movements, repositioning the pliers as necessary, than to attempt to make one continuous circle. Repeat Steps 2–4 to form another link at the other end of the bead.

Neatening ends

When you've wrapped one piece of wire around another—when making a clasp, for example—it's important to neaten the ends to prevent any sharp pieces from sticking out and snagging on clothing or scratching the wearer.

1 Snip the wire as close as possible to the stem, and then press it firmly with your flat- or chain-nose pliers to flatten it against the piece of jewelry. For an extra smooth finish, use a small needle file or sandpaper to file away any roughness.

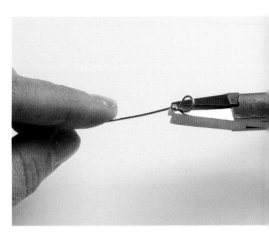

Making a head pin

If you want to suspend a bead from a chain, you only need a suspension link at one end of the bead. At the other end, you need to make what is known as a "head pin," which is virtually invisible but prevents the bead from slipping off the wire.

The head pin (on the right-hand end of the bead) is unobtrusive, but it prevents the bead from slipping off the wire.

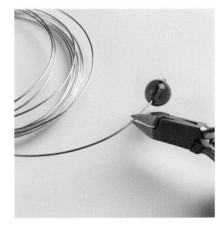

1 Working from the spool, thread your chosen bead onto the wire and let it slip down, leaving the end exposed.

2 Using the tips of your round-nose pliers, make a tiny curl at one end of the wire. Squeeze this curl flat with your flat-nose pliers to create a knob of doubled wire.

You can also make decorative head pins. From left to right: wire curled into a closed spiral; wire hammered so that it spreads in a "feather" shape; seed bead threaded onto the wire above the head pin.

3 Push your bead right up to the "head pin" and snip the wire, leaving a stem about ½ in. (1 cm) long. Form a link at this end of the wire, using your round-nose pliers. If the hole in the bead is large and it slips over the head pin, bend the head pin at a right angle, so that the bead sits on top of it like a tiny shelf. (Alternatively, slide on a small seed bead to act as a stopper.)

Making spirals

There are two kinds of spiral: open and closed. Each is formed in the same way, the only difference being whether or not any space is left between the coils. Both types of spiral begin by curling a circle at the end of the wire. If you want to make a closed spiral without a center hole, make a head pin first and curl the remaining wire around the doubled-up end.

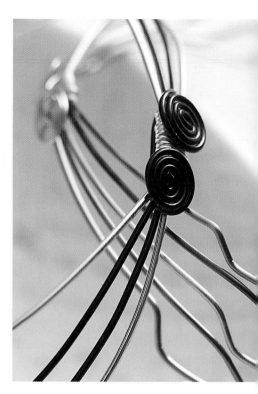

A closed spiral has no gaps between the coils.

An open spiral is made in the same way, but evenly spaced gaps are left between the coils.

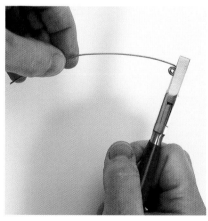

1 Begin by curling a small circle at the end of the wire, using the tips of your round-nose pliers. Make this circle as round as possible, as the rest of the spiral will be shaped around it.

2 Grip the circle tightly in the jaws of your flat-nose pliers and begin curling the wire around it. For a closed spiral, shown here, butt each coil up tightly against the previous one. For an open spiral, leave space between one coil and the next, making sure that the spaces are even.

3 When the spiral is the size you want, leave about ½ in. (1 cm) of wire to form a suspension link, curling the projecting end of wire into a small loop in the opposite direction to the spiral.

Spiral S-link

This timeless chain linking system is simple and stylish and will turn any suspended bead necklace into a decorative masterpiece.

The completed spiral S-link.

Here, spiral S-links have been connected together into a chain, using a pair of jump rings (see page 16) between each two units to add extra security. If you want to add color to the chain, thread a bead onto your cut wire in Step 1 and create the spiral S-shape around it.

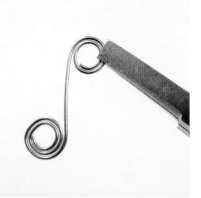

1 Cut 4 in. (10 cm) of 20-gauge (0.8mm) wire. Curl a large circle at each end, around the widest part of the shaft of your round-nose pliers. The circles should curl in opposite directions.

2 Using your flat-nose pliers, curl each end of the wire inward in a tight spiral until they meet in the center.

Using a jig

Before you try a jig project, place your pegs in your chosen design and then wrap a piece of cord or string approximately the same gauge as the wire that will be used around the pegs, following the pattern. Measure the amount of cord or string that you have used so that you know how much wire you will need to make the project, and then cut your wire to this length. To work harden your jig unit, flatten it in your flat-nose pliers or gently "stroke" hammer (see page 20) the outer extremities of the motif.

1 Following your chosen pattern, place the pegs in the jig. Using your round-nose pliers, form a link at one end of your length of wire and slip it over the first peg, securing it in place.

2 Pull the wire around the pegs, following the pattern. You will need to keep pushing the wire down to the base of the pegs in order to keep the motif reasonably flat. Carefully remove the wire unit from the pegs so that it doesn't spring out of shape. If you have wire left over when you've made the unit, simply snip it off.

Making jump rings

Jump rings are used to connect units together. You can buy them ready-made, but it is well worth learning how to make them yourself as you can then match the jump rings to the color and size of wire that you are using. It is also much less expensive to make them yourself!

Jump rings are made by forming a wire coil around the shaft of your round-nose pliers, out of which you snip individual rings as required. When you bring the wire around the pliers to begin forming the second ring of the coil, it needs to go below the first coil, nearer your hand. This keeps the wire on the same part of the pliers every time. If you bring the wire around and above the first ring of the coil, the jump rings will taper, following the shape of the pliers' shaft. You can also make jump rings by wrapping wire around a cylindrical object such as a knitting needle, large nail, or the barrel of a pen, depending on the diameter required.

Jump rings can also be linked together to create a chain. From top to bottom: silver jump rings linked together; copper jump rings interspersed with pairs of smaller silver jump rings; copper jump rings.

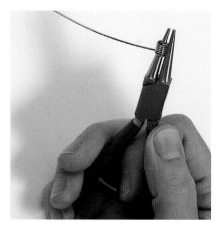

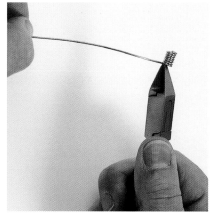

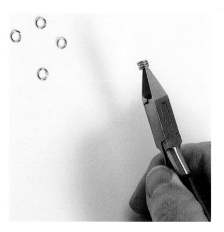

1 Working from the spool, wrap wire five or six times around one shaft of your round-nose pliers, curling it around the same part of the pliers every time to create an even coil.

2 Remove the coil from the pliers and cut if off from the spool of wire using your wire cutters.

3 Find the cut end and, using your wire cutters, snip upward into the next ring of the coil above, thereby cutting off a full circle. Continue cutting each ring off the coil in turn to obtain more jump rings.

Using jump rings to connect units

Jump rings are used to connect units together; they can also be joined together to make a chain.

To toughen (or work harden) the jump rings, carefully move the two ends of the ring just past one another (holding one side with your flat-nose pliers and the other side with your chain-nose pliers); this manipulation will provide tension, enabling the cut ends to sit more securely together. Spend a little extra time checking that there are no gaps between your links, so that when you come to wear the piece you know it won't all fall apart. For extra security and peace of mind, link units together with two or three jump rings instead of just one.

Using your flat-nose pliers, open one of the jump rings sideways (like a door), so that you do not distort the shape. Loop the open jump ring through the links of the beads or individual chain units and close it with flat-nose pliers.

Fish-hook clasp

The most commonly used clasp is the fish-hook, which is also one of the simplest to create.

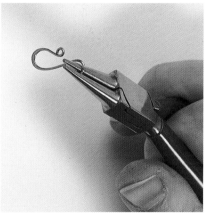

This hook-shaped clasp is both decorative and functional.

1 Working directly from a spool of wire, curl the end of the wire into a small loop, using the tips of your round-nose pliers. Reposition your pliers on the other side of the wire, just under the loop, and curl the wire in the opposite direction around the wider part of the pliers to form the fish-hook clasp.

2 Cut the wire off the spool, leaving about ½ in. (1 cm) to form a link (see page 12). If you wish, you can gently hammer the hook on a steel stake to work harden and flatten it slightly, thereby making it stronger and more durable.

Doubled fish-hook clasp

This fastener is much sturdier than a basic fish-hook clasp, as a double thickness of wire is used. You will need to cut at least 3 in. (7.5 cm) of wire.

The double thickness of wire makes this a much sturdier clasp for necklaces and bracelets—particularly if they contain relatively heavy beads that might put a strain on an ordinary clasp.

1 Find the center of the wire and bend the wire around the tips of your round-nose pliers.

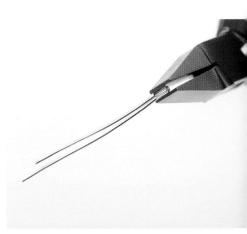

2 Using your round-nose pliers, squeeze the folded end of the wires together and carefully straighten them out with your fingers, so that they run parallel to one another.

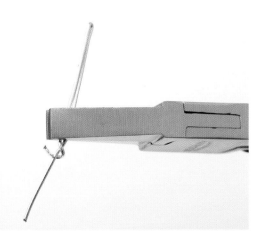

3 Leaving about 1 in. (2.5 cm) of doubled wire, wrap one wire two or three times around the other. Snip off any excess wrapped wire, leaving the other stem of wire extending.

4 Curl the doubled wire around the shaft of your round-nose pliers into a hook shape. Again using your round-nose pliers, curl the very tip of the hook up into a small "lip."

5 Complete the clasp by forming a link (see page 12) at the opposite end of the single protruding wire. (For extra color and decoration, you can add a bead before forming your link.)

Toggle clasp

This simple T-shaped clasp is particularly useful on bracelets, as it is more secure than a fish-hook clasp. The eye fastener needs to be larger than usual to fit the "T" or toggle bar; use a large knitting needle or nail to form the loop.

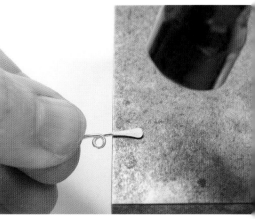

1 To make the T-bar part of the clasp, cut 1 in. (2.5 cm) of 20-gauge (0.8mm) wire. Place your round-nose pliers in the center of the wire and curl the wire around them to make a complete loop. Straighten out the wire on either side of the loop so that it projects out at each side in a straight line.

2 Hammer (see page 20) each projecting end of wire on a steel stake, spreading the metal out at each end—but do not touch the central loop.

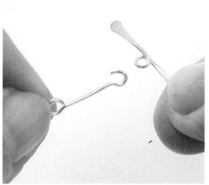

3 To make the toggle stem, cut 1 in. (2.5 cm) of wire and, using the tips of your round-nose pliers, form a small link (see page 12) at each end.

4 Open up one link of the stem, and connect it into the central loop of the T-bar that you made in Step 1. Close the link again. Connect the other link of the stem to the bracelet in the same way.

The completed T-bar clasp. For a more decorative version of this clasp, cut 2 in. (5 cm) of 20-gauge (0.8mm) wire, curl a tight spiral at each side of the center loop created in Step 1, and omit Step 2 altogether.

The "eye" of the fastener

This "eye" can be used to complete all the clasps shown above.

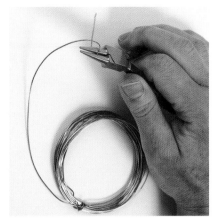

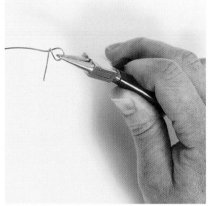

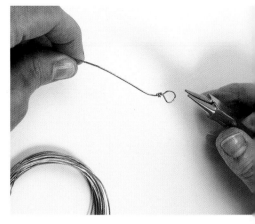

1 Working from the spool, curl a piece of wire around the widest part of your round-nose pliers about 1 in. (2.5 cm) from the end of the wire to form a loop, crossing the end of the wire over itself.

2 Wrap the extending wire around the stem, just under the loop, to secure.

3 Cut the wire off the spool, leaving ½ in. (1 cm) extending. Squeeze the cut end flat against the stem, making sure no spiky ends protrude. Using round-nose pliers, form a link with the extending wire (see page 12).

4 Gently hammer the "eye" on a steel stake to flatten and toughen it. Do not hammer the wires that have been wrapped over the stem or you will weaken them.

The "eye" can be linked to the ends of a necklace or bracelet directly or via jump rings.

Work hardening

Work hardening means toughening the wire so that it can take the strain of being worn without distorting and falling apart. One method is to hammer the piece on a clean, smooth, dent-free steel stake (see page 8). Use a nylon hammer or place a cloth over the piece before you hammer when work hardening colored wire, as the colored coating can rub off. This technique is not suitable for small jump rings or links, as it will distort their shape; see page 17 for how to strengthen jump rings.

Place your piece on the stake and "stroke" hammer it, bringing the flat part of the hammer down at 90° to the piece. Hammer your piece standing up, so that the hammer head hits the wire squarely, rather than at an angle, which could create texturing in the metal. After several strokes you will see the wire flattening, spreading, and work hardening.

Coiled fish-hook clasp and fastener

This fish-hook clasp is used on cord, rope, leather, or ribbon—in fact, on anything to which a jump ring or hook cannot be attached.

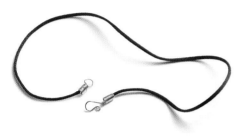

The completed coiled fish-hook clasp and fastener. To make a coiled fastener for two or three ribbons or cords, wrap masking tape around the ends before you slide the coil over them.

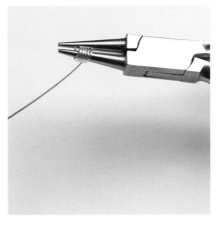

1 Working from the spool, make two coils of wire about ¼ in. (5mm) long, in the same way as when making jump rings (see page 16). Check that the cord or rope you are using can fit snugly into the center of the coil.

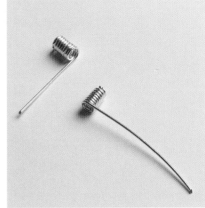

2 Cut the wire off the spool, leaving a 1-in. (2.5-cm) tail of wire on one coil and 1½-in. (4-cm) tail on the other. For added security, dab Superglue inside the coil before you insert the ribbon or cord.

3 At the end of the longer wire, form a fish-hook clasp (see page 17) without a suspension link. Using your flat-nose pliers, turn the hook at 90° to the coil.

4 At the end of the shorter wire, curl your wire around the widest part of your round-nose pliers so that it sits perpendicular to the coil, thus forming the "eye" of the fastener. I recommend hammering the ends of both the fish-hook clasp and the eye fastener on a steel stake to strengthen them, but this is optional. Do not, of course, hammer the coils!

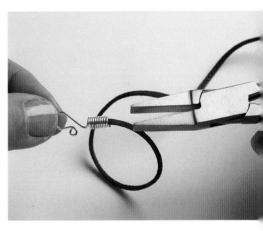

5 Insert the cord or ribbon into the coil. Press the last ring of the coil tightly against the cord with the tips of your flat-nose pliers, so that the fastener is held securely in place.

Chapter 1
bijoux bangles

A beautiful bangle is a simple, yet eye-catching, way of making a style statement but, as these projects show, even apparently complicated pieces can be made without breaking the bank. Ranging from delicate twists of silver wire threaded onto a simple frame to a chunky elasticated design incorporating old buttons as "charms," the projects in this chapter are "arm candy" of the highest order!

bolt 'n' bead bangle

The matt surface of the hexagonal bolts provides a striking contrast to the shininess of the beads. This bangle illustrates how you can use a simple piece of household equipment to create a unique piece of jewelry. Other items from your local hardware store, such as steel washers or short pieces of plastic tubing, can be used between the beads as spacers; see the Washer Sundial Choker on page 102.

you will need

20-gauge (0.8mm) silver wire

13 x 10mm plastic faceted "crystal" beads

12 steel bolts, approx. ½ in. (12–14mm) in diameter

Wire cutters

Round- and flat-nose pliers

Hammer and steel stake (optional)

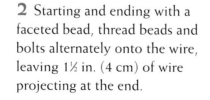

1 Cut 10 in. (25 cm) of 20-gauge (0.8mm) silver wire. Make a wrapped loop (see page 20) at one end for the "eye" of the fastener. If you wish, "stroke" hammer the rounded end on a steel stake to work harden it (see page 20).

2 Starting and ending with a faceted bead, thread beads and bolts alternately onto the wire, leaving 1½ in. (4 cm) of wire projecting at the end.

3 Bend the projecting wire in two and wrap the end around the stem, just under the last threaded bead. Neaten the end (see page 13). Make a fish-hook clasp (see page 17) at the end of the doubled wire.

4 Wrap the piece around a cylindrical object that is slightly smaller in diameter than the bangle and press it around to create the circular shape. Spend a little time shaping it.

RIGHT For a lighter-looking design, place thin coils of wire between the bolts and beads. I used silver coils to match the steely gray color of the other elements.

Bolt 'n' Bead Bangle **25**

ribbon-weave bangle

If you're a dressmaker, here's your chance to design a bangle to match your outfit, using leftover fabric. Alternatively, make a fabric cuff from leftover ribbon. I can also imagine this design being made from a piece of pretty lace, embroidered with seed beads, for a wedding band.

you will need

12-gauge (2mm) and 20-gauge (0.8mm) silver wire

Ribbon of your choice, 1 in. (2.5 cm) wide

Double-sided tape

Heavy-duty and standard wire cutters

Round- and flat-nose pliers

Hammer and steel stake (optional)

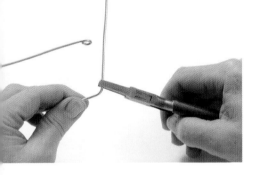

1 Using heavy-duty cutters, cut 19 in. (48 cm) of 12-gauge (2mm) silver wire. Using flat-nose pliers, bend the wire at 90°, 7 in. (18 cm) from one end, and then again 1 in. (2.5 cm) farther along, to make a U-shape with one side 4 in. (10 cm) longer than the other. Form a link (see page 12) at the shorter end of the U-shape.

2 Push the longer end through the link to make a rectangular frame for the bangle, then bend the link so that it sits at 90° to the frame. Form the end of the wire into an open spiral (see page 14) and flatten the spiral against the frame.

3 Using your hands, shape the wire around a bottle or jar to form a circular bangle. If you own a nylon-headed hammer, gently tap the wire frame to work harden it; if you're using a metal hammer, "stroke" hammer (see page 20) the wire with care.

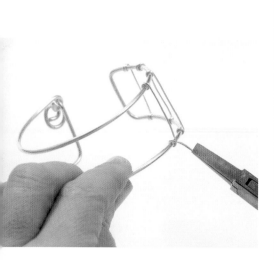

4 Using standard wire cutters, cut twelve 2½-in. (6.5-cm) lengths of 20-gauge (0.8mm) silver wire. Center each wire vertically on the frame, then use your flat-nose pliers to wrap it around the frame, top and bottom. Neaten the ends (see page 13). Slide the wires around the frame until you have six evenly spaced pairs.

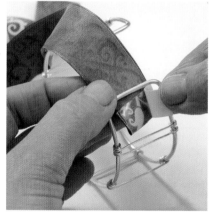

5 Cut a sliver of double-sided tape and stick it to the cut end of the ribbon. Fold the end of the ribbon over onto the sticky surface to make a hem; this will prevent the end of the ribbon from fraying.

6 Stick another sliver of double-side tape over the "hemmed" end of ribbon. Feed the ribbon under the end of the wire frame from the back, peel off the backing paper from the tape, fold the sticky tab of ribbon over the frame, and press down to secure the ribbon around the bangle frame.

7 Weave the ribbon through each pair of wires, feeding it under the first wire and over the second wire of each pair, until you reach the end of the bangle. Cut the ribbon, leaving 1 in. (2.5 cm) projecting. Repeat Steps 5 and 6 to secure the end of the ribbon around the bangle frame, making sure the ribbon is pulled straight and taut.

balcony bangle

Wrought-iron balconies inspired me to make this delicate-looking bangle, with its twisted-wire spindles. Once you've mastered the technique, it can be made with threaded buttons or with threaded beads for added color. You could also increase the diameter to make a stunning choker necklace.

you will need

20-gauge (0.8mm) silver wire

80 x 4mm round silver beads

Wire cutters

Round-, chain-, and flat-nose pliers

Hammer and steel stake

1 Cut two 7-in. (17.5-cm) lengths of 20-gauge (0.8mm) silver wire. At one end of each wire, curl the wire once around one shaft of your round-nose pliers to form a link (see page 12).

2 Cut about forty 1½-in. (4-cm) lengths for the vertical twists. Form a link (see page 12) at each end of each wire. "Stroke" hammer (see page 20) the wire between the links to flatten the stems, taking care not to hammer the links.

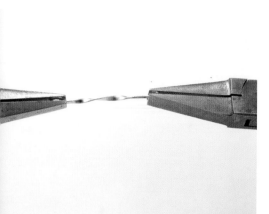

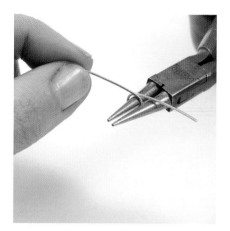

3 Hold one end of each hammered wire very firmly in your chain-nose pliers and the other end in your flat-nose pliers. Gently turn one hand to form a twist in the flattened wire stem.

4 Thread a twisted wire onto the 7-in. (17.5-cm) lengths, pushing it right up to the links. Thread a 4mm bead onto each wire of the frame. Repeat, alternating twisted wires and beads. Using round-nose pliers, form a link (see page 12) at the end of the top and bottom wires, turning the links inward so that they face each other.

5 Cut two 2-in. (5-cm) lengths of 20-gauge (0.8mm) wire. Place your round-nose pliers at the center of each wire and curl the wire around until it crosses over, forming a loop. Make one loop larger than the other, as this will be the "eye" of the fastener.

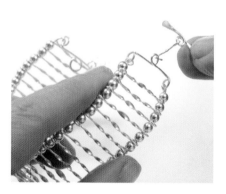

6 Form a link (see page 12) at each end of each length. Using flat-nose pliers, bend the links at 90° to the main shaft, so that they face each other. "Stroke" hammer each length (see page 20) to work harden it.

7 Open up the links and attach one piece to each end of the bangle.

8 Make a toggle clasp (see page 19). Open up the jump ring at the base of the fastener, loop it through the end piece with the smaller center loop, and close it again to complete the piece.

RIGHT To vary the design, incorporate threaded beads or buttons (as shown here). The buttons are held in place with wire coils created in the same way as jump rings (see page 16).

stretchy charm bracelet

Charm bracelets are always popular—the more heavily laden, the better! Here, buttons, beads, hammered scraps of leftover wire, and even caged shells and tiny pebbles, are attached to a length of chain from a home improvements store, to create a really eye-catching piece of contemporary jewelry from virtually nothing. You need to use a chunky chain with large links, so that you can thread elastic through in order to gather the chain.

you will need

20-gauge (0.8mm) wire

0.5mm clear elastic

Approx. 28 in. (70 cm) colored 8mm curb chain

Beads or charms of your choice

Wire cutters

Round- and flat-nose pliers

Superglue

1 Cut 1 in. (2.5 cm) of 20-gauge (0.8mm) wire and curl a tiny hook at one end. Tie a 10-in. (25-cm) length of clear elastic around the hook, leaving about 1 in. (2.5 cm) projecting, then squeeze the hook with your pliers. Weave the wire in and out of the links of the curb chain like a needle, gathering the chain as you go.

2 When you reach the end of the chain, thread the elastic through to the very first link and tie a knot with both ends of the elastic to create the bracelet shape. Tie the elastic three or four times and place a tiny dab of Superglue on the knot for extra security.

3 Thread your chosen buttons, beads, hammered wire shapes, and charms onto 20-gauge (0.8mm) wire, forming a head pin at one end and a link at the other (see pages 13 and 12).

4 Make the required number of jump rings (see page 16) from 20-gauge (0.8mm) wire. Attach the charms to the chain, spacing them evenly.

wavy wiggles bangle

Here's a simple bangle framework that you can make with colored or twisted wires. If you want to give the bangle more weight and substance, add beads to the ends instead of making the spiral-shaped terminals shown here. The design also looks stunning as a napkin ring, although you would need less wire for this.

you will need
18-gauge (1mm) silver and black wire
24-gauge (0.6mm) silver wire
Masking tape
Wire cutters
Round- and flat-nose pliers
Cylindrical mandrel

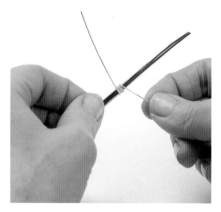

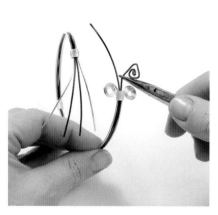

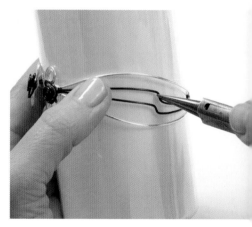

1 Cut two black and two silver 12-in. (30-cm) lengths of 18-gauge (1mm) wire. Bundle them together, with the silver wires on the outside. Wrap slivers of masking tape around the center of the bundle and 2 in. (5 cm) from each end. Wrap 24-gauge (0.6mm) silver wire around each taped area to cover the masking tape. Neaten any cut ends (see page 13).

2 Wrap the wires around a mandrel slightly smaller than your wrist diameter to obtain a bangle shape. Fan the wires out at each end and form each into a closed spiral (see page 14) or irregular "doodle" shape. Spiral the wire right up to the bound wire ends, then press the black "doodles" flat onto the wrapped wire to hide the binding underneath.

3 Using your fingers, pull the wires apart on each side of the central binding. Place the bangle back on the mandrel. Holding the round-nose pliers vertically, place the tips on the black center wires and twist to create wavy lines and wiggles in the wire.

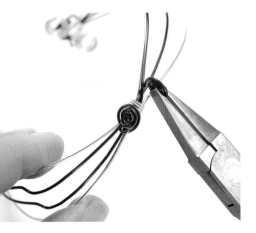

4 Cut 4 in. (10 cm) of 18-gauge (1mm) black wire. Form a closed spiral (see page 14) on each end, leaving about 1 in. (2.5 cm) of straight wire at the center of the spirals, and place this behind the center binding of the bangle. Using flat-nose pliers, fold the spirals over to the front of the bangle and flatten them against the binding wire underneath.

Chapter 2
ravishing rings

A handcrafted ring is perhaps the simplest and most inexpensive way of matching your jewelry to your outfit as, with a cluster of just a few tiny recycled beads or even a single prettily shaped button, you can coordinate the colors to perfection. The projects in this chapter allow you to experiment not only with different bead combination centerpieces, but also with different ways of creating ring shanks, from simple overlapping loops and colored coils to more intricate wire-wrapping.

beaded bird-nest ring

You can use this design to use up any odd beads you have lying around, or use semi-precious chips as I have done. The nest of wire around the beads highlights whatever is within it—like precious bird eggs. Even though this ring looks extravagant, it's relatively cheap to make and can be the perfect birthday present if you use the recipient's birthstone.

you will need

26-gauge (0.4mm) and 20-gauge (0.8mm) silver wire

6–8 small semi-precious chips in assorted colors

Wire cutters

Round- and flat-nose pliers

Hammer and steel stake

Ring mandrel

1 Measure the circumference of the ring size required, double this measurement, and add 2 in. (5 cm). Cut a piece of 20-gauge (0.8mm) silver wire to this length. Place your round-nose pliers at the center of the wire and wrap both ends around one of the tapered shafts, until they cross over each other and the ends project in opposite directions.

2 Keeping the wire in place on the pliers, wrap the wire ends around the second shaft, crossing them over as before, to form a second loop.

3 Reposition the pliers so that the first shaft of the pliers is threaded through the last loop and cross the wires over so that the ends project in opposite directions, as before.

4 Continue creating a looped band, repositioning your pliers each time, until the band is the length you require. Pull one wire out straight, so that it's parallel to the loops. Using flat-nose pliers, wrap the other wire around this stem. Cut off any excess and neaten the end (see page 13), leaving the first wire projecting.

5 Bend the looped band around to form a circle, threading the projecting wire through the first loop that you made in Step 2. Form a link (see page 12) at the end of the projecting wire to complete the ring shank.

6 If the band seems very uneven, gently stroke it flat with a hammer on a steel block and then wrap it around the ring mandrel to shape it. Gently "stroke" hammer it (see page 20) on the ring mandrel to work harden it.

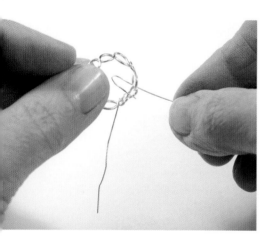
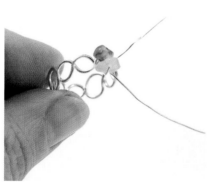

7 Cut 3–4 in. (8–10 cm) of 26-gauge (0.4mm) wire. Wrap the center of this wire around the looped band, at the point where you formed the securing link in Step 5, leaving both ends of wire protruding.

8 Thread the end of each wire in turn with semi-precious chips, placing the colors randomly and wrapping the wire around the ring shank after every two or three stones to secure them in place. The stones will hide the area where the two ends of the ring join.

9 When all the stones are on, wrap the wire ends around the ring shank, snip off any excess, and neaten the ends at the back of the ring (see page 13).

11 Put the ring back on the mandrel. Wrap the rest of the spiraled wire around the outer edge of the chips to create the "nest." When you run out of wire, push the end into the back of the shank, securing and hiding it in amongst the chips. To make a larger nest, repeat Steps 10–11, wrapping another length of wire around to frame the chips.

10 Cut 10 in. (25 cm) of 20-gauge (0.8mm) wire. Form a tiny closed spiral (see page 14) at one end. Hook the end of the spiral into the area of wire where the chips are wrapped, between the ring shank and the stones, making sure it's secure and wedged in.

Beaded Bird-nest Ring **41**

pretty button ring

you will need

20-gauge (0.8mm) and 26-gauge (0.4mm) silver wire

Feature button

1 x 4mm round silver bead

Wire cutters

Round- and flat-nose pliers

Ring mandrel

Hammer

This ring is very simple to make and has an adjustable shank, so it should fit most sizes of finger. Make it to match a new outfit, as most new garments are sold with a couple of spare buttons that are usually left forgotten at the back of a drawer.

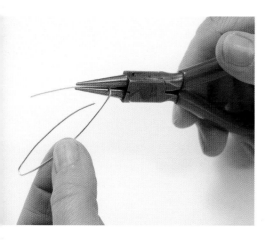

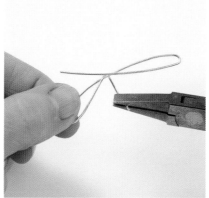

1 Cut about 6 in. (15 cm) of 20-gauge (0.8mm) silver wire. Using round-nose pliers, bend each end of the wire in toward the center, about 1½ in. (4 cm) from the ends.

2 Wrap both ends of the wire around the center of the wire to secure, forming two even-sized loops. Cut off any excess and neaten the ends (see page 13).

3 Press the wire piece around the ring mandrel to form the ring shape. Gently hammer the rounded ends to flatten and work harden the piece (see page 20).

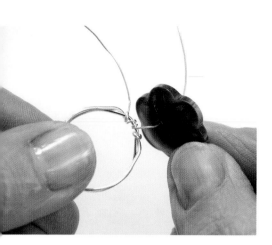 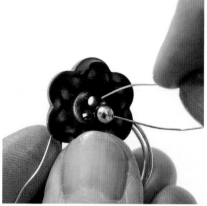 

4 Cut about 3 in. (7.5 cm) of 26-gauge (0.4mm) silver wire. Wrap the center of the wire around the center of the ring shank. Feed the button onto one of the extending wires.

5 Thread on the silver bead, then feed the wire back through the second button hole.

6 Wrap both ends of the wire around, under the button, to secure. Cut off any excess and neaten the ends (see page 13).

two-tone doodle ring

The "doodle" bead at the center of the ring is a coil of wire with another length of wire wrapped around it in a random fashion—just as you might absent-mindedly doodle an abstract design on a piece of paper. I've been making wire beads for a while, but usually to suspend from necklaces—this is my first ring in this style. It is perhaps not as decorative as the other rings in this chapter, but with the use of colored wire it can look contemporary and fun! It also looks great (and quite masculine) made entirely in silver and then treated with liver of sulfur to blacken it and create an antique effect.

you will need

20-gauge (0.8mm) silver and colored wire
Wire cutters
Round- and flat-nose pliers
Hammer and steel stake
Ring mandrel

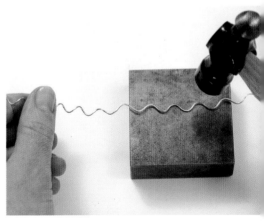

1 Make a small coil of 20-gauge (0.8mm) silver wire about ½ in. (1 cm) long, in the same way as when making jump rings (see page 16). Pull the first and last loop of the coil out and, using your flat-nose pliers, twist them so that they sit at 90° to the coil and form links.

2 Holding the links in your pliers, stretch the coil out until it's about ¾ in. (2 cm) long.

3 Make another coil of 20-gauge (0.8mm) silver wire, this time about 1 in. (2.5 cm) in length. Pull each end of the coil and stretch it out completely. Hammer lightly along the length to create a flat, wavy wire.

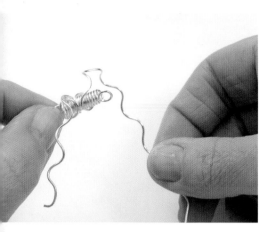

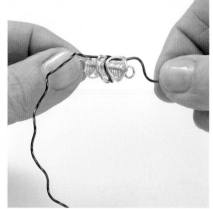

4 Find the center of this wavy wire and wrap it around the center of the coil you created in Step 1. When all the wire has been used up, push the ends into the coil so that they don't protrude.

5 Make another 1-in. (2.5-cm) coil, this time using colored wire. Repeat Steps 3 and 4, wrapping it over the wavy silver wire. If you feel the "doodle" bead doesn't look full enough, repeat Steps 3 and 4, wrapping more wire around the bead to make a larger unit.

6 To make the shank of the ring, cut about 3½ in. (9 cm) of 20-gauge (0.8mm) wire and bend it around your mandrel to create a U-shape, with the ends projecting straight out. Make a small even coil of colored wire about 2 in. (5 cm) long. Thread the coil over the U-shaped wire, positioning it at the center of the curve.

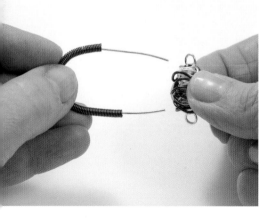

7 Thread the end links projecting on each side of the "doodle" bead onto the ends of the U-shaped wire, pushing it right up against the colored coil.

8 Form a small, closed spiral (see page 14) on the end of each projecting wire, spiraling back in toward the ring shank.

9 Using flat-nose pliers, bend the spirals back, so that they sit flat against the ring shank. If necessary, place the ring back on the mandrel and adjust the shape.

ABOVE AND RIGHT This is a very
simple, freeform way of creating
coordinating pieces of jewelry. Here,
to complement the red-and-silver
rings (above), I've used a "doodle"
bead as the focal bead for a pendant,
and added a spiral to the end (right).

cluster ring

Here's a bold, chunky, statement ring—not suitable for wearing when doing the housework, but great made with beads to match an evening outfit! As only a few beads are required, it's a great way of recycling old, broken necklaces. If you want to use smaller beads or semi-precious stones, substitute 24-gauge (0.6mm) wire for the 20-gauge (0.8mm) wire that I used in Step 1—but still use the thicker wire in Step 9 to create a sturdy shank.

you will need

20-gauge (0.8mm) and 24-gauge (0.6mm) silver wire

Approx.8 x 4–6mm beads of your choice

Masking tape

Scissors

Wire cutters

Round- and flat-nose pliers

Hammer

Ring mandrel

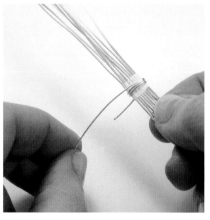

1 Cut four 6-in. (15-cm) lengths of 20-gauge (0.8mm) silver wire. Fold each length in half and squeeze the ends together until the wires are doubled and straightened. Lay the four doubled wires out in a row and tape them together with a sliver of masking tape, leaving only ½ in. (1 cm) of the doubled ends protruding.

2 To hide the taped area, wrap some 24-gauge (0.6mm) silver wire over it.

3 Holding the doubled ends firmly in your flat-nose pliers, bend them over and squeeze tightly to flatten them against the bundle of wires.

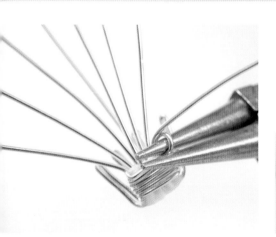

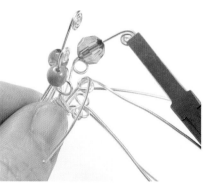

4 Separate the eight projecting ends of wire with your fingers, so that they radiate out like a fan. Use the tips of your round-nose pliers to curl a small loop in each of the projecting wires, near the taped area.

5 Thread a bead onto each projecting length, pushing it down the wire so that it sits close to the loop you made in Step 4. Form a closed spiral (see page 14) on the end of each wire, curling it right up to the bead to secure it in place.

6 Using round-nose pliers, form the doubled-over wires into four small links (see page 12).

FAR LEFT The long wire that forms the ring shank is wrapped around the base of the beaded cluster to provide a rigid support.

LEFT Spirals hold the beads firmly in place and form a decorative feature in their own right.

RIGHT Faceted beads catch the light, while their sharp angles contrast well with the flowing lines of the silver spirals.

7 Cut about 12 in. (30 cm) of 20-gauge (0.8mm) wire and thread it through the doubled wire links.

8 Place the unit on a ring mandrel, with the beaded cluster at the center of the wire, and wrap the wire around so that the ends project out on each side of the beaded cluster. Wrap one of the projecting wires around the base of the cluster in one direction and the other over the top of the cluster in the opposite direction. Continue until you've used up all the wire.

9 Push the ends of the wire into the cluster, making sure no ends stick out. Using your fingers, flatten the beaded cluster against the shank. Spend a little time rearranging the front of the ring into an aesthetic arrangement. Gently "stroke" hammer (see page 20) the back of the ring shank on the mandrel to toughen and temper the wire.

wrapped embrace ring

This is a fun ring and a great way to use up small beads of the same color but different tones and hues. Only one length of wire is required, which "embraces" all the beads plus the shank—hence its title! For bead color combination and inspiration, why not pick them out from your favorite fabric, carpet design, or even wrapping paper?

you will need

20-gauge (0.8mm) silver wire

About 10 mixed beads, 3–7mm in size

Wire cutters

Round- and flat-nose pliers

Hammer

Ring mandrel

1 Cut about 10 in. (25 cm) of 20-gauge (0.8mm) silver wire. Hold the wire firmly against the ring mandrel, leaving about 1 in. (2.5 cm) projecting, and wrap it around to make one complete loop. Bring the wire halfway around the mandrel, and then thread on two or three small beads. Wrap the wire tightly around the mandrel again to form a second complete loop.

2 Repeat Step 1 twice more to create two additional loops, adding three or four more beads of various sizes and colors. Make sure all the beads are positioned together at the front of the loops, above each other in rows, and then carefully slide the loops off the mandrel.

3 Secure the cut ends of wire by wrapping the wire around all the loops, on each side of the beads. Cut off any excess wire and neaten the ends (see page 13).

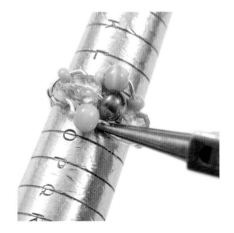

4 Place the ring on the mandrel and "stroke" hammer the back and sides (see page 20), taking care not to hammer the beads. Place the tips of your round-nose pliers between any of the beads and twist the wire to toughen it; this will also produce a more interesting pattern at the front. Remember: the more you twist the wires, the smaller the ring will become.

Chapter 3
elegant earrings

Earrings instantly add drama and a touch of feminine glamor to any outfit, whether it's for day- or eveningwear. As they're on a small scale, all these earring projects are relatively quick to make and provide the ideal opportunity to hone your wire-working skills. And, as you need only a few beads to make a pair of earrings, this is the perfect opportunity to recycle broken necklaces or second-hand bracelets into brand-new fashion statements.

Candelabras are synonymous with sparkling elegance and style, so I used crystal beads for these earrings. Crystal and pearl combinations would make very pretty wedding earrings; alternatively, try black crystals on gold wire for stunning eveningwear.

you will need

20-gauge (0.8mm) silver wire

2 x 10mm, 2 x 6mm, and 4 x 8mm bicone blue crystals

2 x 4mm round silver beads

2 x ready-made ear wires

Wire cutters

Masking tape

Round-, chain-, and flat-nose pliers

Hammer and steel stake

1 For each earring, cut one 2½-in. (6.5-cm) and four 2-in. (5-cm) lengths of 20-gauge (0.8mm) silver wire. Place all the wires together in a bunch and secure with a sliver of masking tape, with all the wires aligning at one end and the long wire sticking out at the other end.

2 Using round-nose pliers and working from the spool of wire, make a coil of 20-gauge (0.8mm) wire just long enough to cover the masking tape, in the same way as when making jump rings (see page 16). Slide the coil over the end of the bunch of wires to hide the masking tape.

3 Using chain-nose pliers, squeeze the first and last loops of the coil to secure it tightly around the bunch of wires.

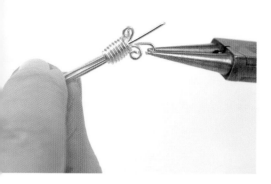  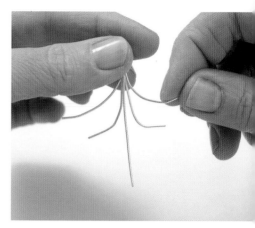

4 Above the coil, using the tips of your round-nose pliers, curl the end of each short wire into a small spiral. Using flat-nose pliers, flatten the spirals against the coil.

5 Curl the end of the long wire into a link (see page 12).

6 Below the coil, curl each short wire outward by wrapping it around a cylindrical object such as a pencil and then adjusting the shape with your fingers. Leave the long central wire uncurled.

 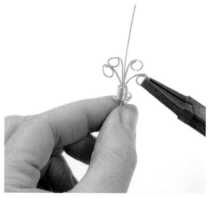 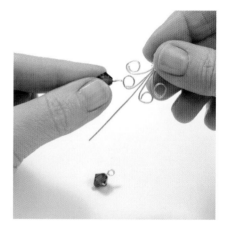

7 Using your round-nose pliers, curl the end of each short wire into a large circle.

8 Using flat-nose pliers, curl the circles around a little more so the ends overlap—as if starting a spiral (see page 14).

9 Thread four 8mm bicone crystals (two for each earring) with wire, forming a link at one end and a head pin at the other (see pages 12 and 13). Open up the links and hook them over the bottom two circles on each earring. Close the links again with flat-nose pliers.

RIGHT *For a slightly more elaborate and glitzy look, add an extra clear glass bead above the coiled stem and suspend a drop bead from a jump ring at the base of the "candelabra."*

10 Thread the remaining beads onto the long center wire in this order: 10mm bicone crystal, 6mm bicone crystal, 4mm silver bead. Form a head pin (see page 13) at the end of the wire to hold the beads in place.

11 To connect the units to ready-made ear wires, open the link at the bottom of the ear wire, hook it into the link at the top of the "candelabra," and close with flat-nose pliers.

starburst earrings

Inspired by Indian "Bollywood" style, these hoop earrings look exotic and flamboyant, with the "dangles" radiating out from the central star bead like trails of light. The circular pendant can be increased in size to make a matching pendant.

you will need

20-gauge (0.8mm) silver wire

20 x 4mm and 2 x 6mm round silver beads

2 x ½-in. (1-cm) silver star beads

2 x 8mm, 4 x 6mm, and 2 x 4mm purple faceted plastic crystal beads

Assorted purple seed beads

2 x ready-made ear wires

Wire cutters

Round- and flat-nose pliers

Circular mandrel, 1 in. (2.5 cm) in diameter

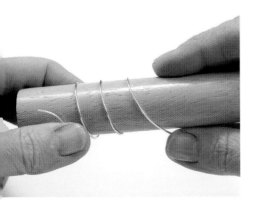

1 Working from a spool of 20-gauge (0.8mm) wire, wrap the wire twice around the mandrel to form two complete circles. (I used a section of wooden curtain pole as my "mandrel," but any cylindrical object the right size will do.)

2 Cut through the coils in the same way as when making jump rings (see page 16), to make two large circles.

3 Cut five lengths of 20-gauge (0.8mm) wire for each earring. I cut two ½-in. (1-cm) lengths for the outer rays, two 2-in. (5-cm) lengths for the inner rays, and one central stem about 3 in. (7.5 cm) long—the length depends on the size of your beads. Thread on your beads, then form one end of the wire into a head pin and the other into a link (see pages 12 and 13).

4 Using round-nose pliers, form a link (see page 12) at one end of each large wire circle.

5 Thread your beads and beaded "rays" onto the circular frames, suspending the long beaded ray in the center of each earring.

6 Using round-nose pliers, form a second link (see page 12) at the other end of the frame. Push the two ends of the frame together, then twist the top links through 90° with your flat-nose pliers, so that they face each other.

  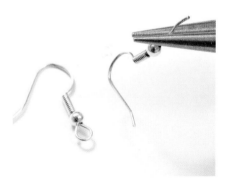

7 Make two small jump rings (see page 16) from 20-gauge (0.8mm) wire. Open them up. Hook each one through the link at the top of a star bead, then close the links tightly with your flat-nose pliers.

8 Make two large jump rings (see page 16) from 20-gauge (0.8mm) wire. Open them up. Hook one through the first link on one circular frame, then through the star bead jump ring, and finally through the second link on the frame. Close the jump ring. Repeat to complete the second earring.

9 Undo the link at the end of the ready-made ear wires, straighten out the wire, and remove any beads.

11 Undo the large jump ring at the top of the starburst piece, hook it through the jump ring at the base of the ear wire, then close the link again with your flat-nose pliers.

10 Slide a 4mm faceted purple crystal bead onto each ear wire, then re-make the link.

LEFT You can suspend any bead or charm at the center of these earrings and create a much simpler design using fewer pendant rays.

teardrop earrings

The tapered shape of this design, with its delicate internal spirals, is very elegant and can be suspended either way up. The "teardrop" unit also looks dramatic as a necklace centerpiece, suspended either from a cord (for a casual look) or from a chain.

you will need

20-gauge (0.8mm) and 26-gauge (0.4mm) silver wire

2 x 10mm gray feature beads

2 x 15mm blue/gray drop pendant beads

2 x 5mm blue/gray round beads

2 x ready-made ear wires

Wire cutters

Round- and flat-nose pliers

Cylindrical mandrel about 1 in. (2.5 cm) in diameter

Hammer and steel stake (optional)

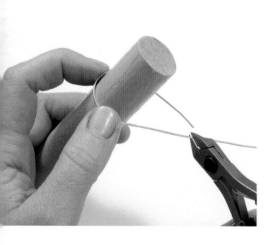

1 For each earring, wrap the end of a spool of 20-gauge (0.8mm) silver wire around a cylindrical mandrel about 1 in. (2.5 cm) in diameter to form a loop, bringing the ends together to a point. Cut the wire to make the teardrop-shaped frame.

2 Wrap one end of the wire around the other, cut off any excess, and neaten the end (see page 13), leaving the second wire projecting. If you wish, gently "stroke" hammer (see page 20) the outer frame to work harden it.

3 Curl the projecting wire into a link (see page 12). This will be the bottom of the earring.

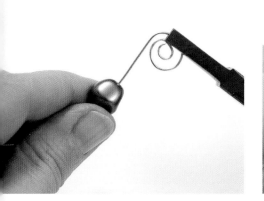

4 Cut two 5–6-in. (12.5–15-cm) lengths of 20-gauge (0.8mm) wire. Thread a feature bead onto each one and form an open spiral (see page 14) on each side, curling the wire in opposite directions like a figure eight. If you wish, "stroke" hammer (see page 20) the spirals, taking care not to hit the central bead.

5 For each earring, cut two 2-in. (5-cm) lengths of 26-gauge (0.4mm) wire. Use each one to bind the spirals to the top and bottom of the teardrop frame. Cut off any excess and neaten the ends (see page 13).

6 Thread the pendant bead onto 20-gauge (0.8mm) wire and form a head pin at one end and a link at the other (see pages 12 and 13). Open the link on the pendant bead, hook it through the link at the base of the teardrop frame, then close the link with your flat-nose pliers.

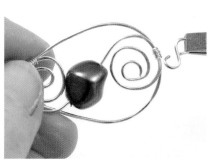
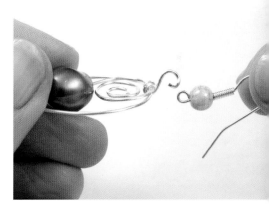

7 Cut a small piece of 20-gauge (0.8mm) wire. Using your round-nose pliers, curl each end into a link (see page 12), curling the wire in opposite directions to form a figure eight.

8 Open one link, hook it under the binding wire at the top of the teardrop frame, then close it again.

9 Undo the link at the end of the ready-made ear wires, straighten out the wire, and remove any beads. Slide a 5mm blue–gray round bead onto each ear wire, then re-make the link. Open the other link on the figure eight made in Step 8, hook it into the bottom link of the ear wire, then close it again.

LEFT Make a pendant necklace to match the earrings by connecting together different-shaped beads in the same steely grays and silvers via jump rings, and suspending a larger version of the teardrop motif from the center.

Teardrop Earrings **67**

bead-pod earrings

This design, which was inspired by flower seeds encased in a papery pod, is ideal for setting off any bicone-shaped beads or crystals that you have in your stash. Framing beads with wire in this way is an effective way of making them more prominent. For something a little more lighthearted, why not use red, orange, and green beads in succession and turn them into "traffic-light" earrings?!

you will need

20-gauge (0.8mm) copper and 26-gauge (0.4mm) gold-plated wire

6 x 6mm bicone crystal beads

2 x 10mm crystal hearts

2 x ready-made earring posts and butterfly backs

Wire cutters

Round-, chain-, and flat-nose pliers

Superglue

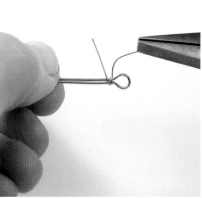

1 For each earring, cut a 5-in. (12.5-cm) length of 20-gauge (0.8mm) copper wire. Placing your round-nose pliers in the center, bend the wire in half. Using the tips of your chain-nose pliers, pinch the wires together just under the round-nose pliers to form a loop, with the projecting wires running parallel to each other.

2 Cut a 1½-in. (4-cm) length of 26-gauge (0.4mm) gold-plated wire and bind it around the doubled wires, just under the loop. Cut off any excess and neaten the end (see page 13).

3 Place your flat-nose pliers by the binding and bend the wire into an angular shape. Continue bending the wire into a zig-zag pattern until you have three complete zig-zags on one side. You should have about ½ in. (1 cm) of wire unbent on each side.

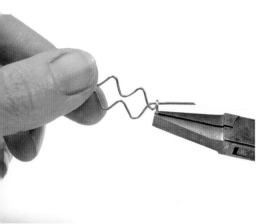

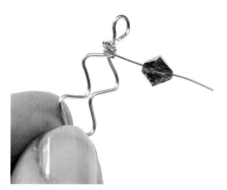

4 Repeat Step 3 on the other wire to create a mirror image of the zig-zags. Straighten one wire stem, then wrap the other wire around that stem to secure. Cut off any excess wire from the wrap, and neaten the end (see page 13).

5 Using your round-nose pliers, form a link (see page 12) at the end of the straight wire.

6 Cut 5 in. (12.5 cm) of 26-gauge (0.4mm) wire. Wrap one end around the binding that you did in Step 2. Using flat-nose pliers, press the end to flatten it against the binding so that no sharp edges protrude. Thread a 6mm bicone crystal onto the wire and position it in the center of the unit, in the space between the first zig-zag.

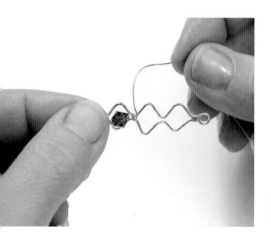

7 Bind again where the two ends of the first zig-zag meet, to secure the bead.

8 Thread your second and third beads onto the frame in the same way, again binding the wire around the frame after each bead. Cut off any excess wire and neaten the end (see page 13).

9 Make a large jump ring from 20-gauge (0.8mm) wire (see page 16). Open the jump ring, hook on a crystal heart, and attach it to one end of the bead pod.

LEFT Note how the wire "pod" is secured by wrapping a finer wire around the end of the earring, just above the final link. A heart-shaped bead provides a glistening finishing touch.

10 Working from the spool of 20-gauge (0.8mm) copper wire, make a closed spiral (see page 14) about ¼ in. (5mm) in diameter. Cut the wire from the spool, leaving about ½–¾ in. (1.5–2 cm) projecting. Curl this projecting wire into a link (see page 12). Using your flat-nose pliers, turn the link so that it sits at 90° to the spiral.

11 Using Superglue, glue the spiral to the flat end of an earring post. Leave the glue to dry completely.

12 Open the link on the spiral, hook it through the link at the opposite end of the bead pod to the crystal heart, and then close the link again to complete the earring.

yin-yang earrings

The curving wire of this design is inspired by the yin-yang symbol, which, in ancient Chinese philosophy, represents the opposing forces that maintain the harmony of the universe. In Chinese culture, jade is considered the most precious of all stones and symbolizes nobility, perfection, constancy, and immortality—so I incorporated jade-green beads and a butterfly pendant into my design to continue the Chinese theme.

you will need

20-gauge (0.8mm) silver wire

4 x 10mm round green beads

2 x 8mm butterfly-shaped beads

2 x ready-made ear posts and butterfly backs

Wire cutters

Round- and flat-nose pliers

Hammer and steel stake

1 For each earring, thread two 10mm beads onto a spool of 20-gauge (0.8mm) silver wire. Wrap the wire twice around the same part of the shaft of your round-nose pliers to make two small coils (see page 16). Push the beads right up to the coils, then form a link (see page 12) at the end of the last threaded bead.

2 Place the widest part of your round-nose pliers by the side of the last threaded bead and form the wire into a curved shape on one side of the bead. (Alternatively, pull the wire into shape using your fingers.) Wrap the wire one and a half times around the stem, in between the two beads.

3 Repeat Step 2 by the side of the first bead that you threaded onto the wire, this time forming the curve on the opposite side. Secure the end of the wire by wrapping it around the top of the stem. Cut the wire off the spool and neaten the end (see page 13). "Stroke" hammer (see page 20) the rounded ends of the curves, being careful not to hammer the beads.

4 Thread one of the small butterfly beads with 20-gauge (0.8mm) wire, forming a link at one end and a head pin at the other (see pages 12 and 13). Open the link, hook it over the link at the base of the earring, then close it again.

5 Using the tips of your flat-nose pliers, carefully separate the two coils at the top of the earring so that they form a V-shape. Make a large jump ring (see page 16) from 20-gauge (0.8mm) wire. Open the jump ring, thread it through the two top coils, and close it again. Connect the earring to a ready-made ear wire.

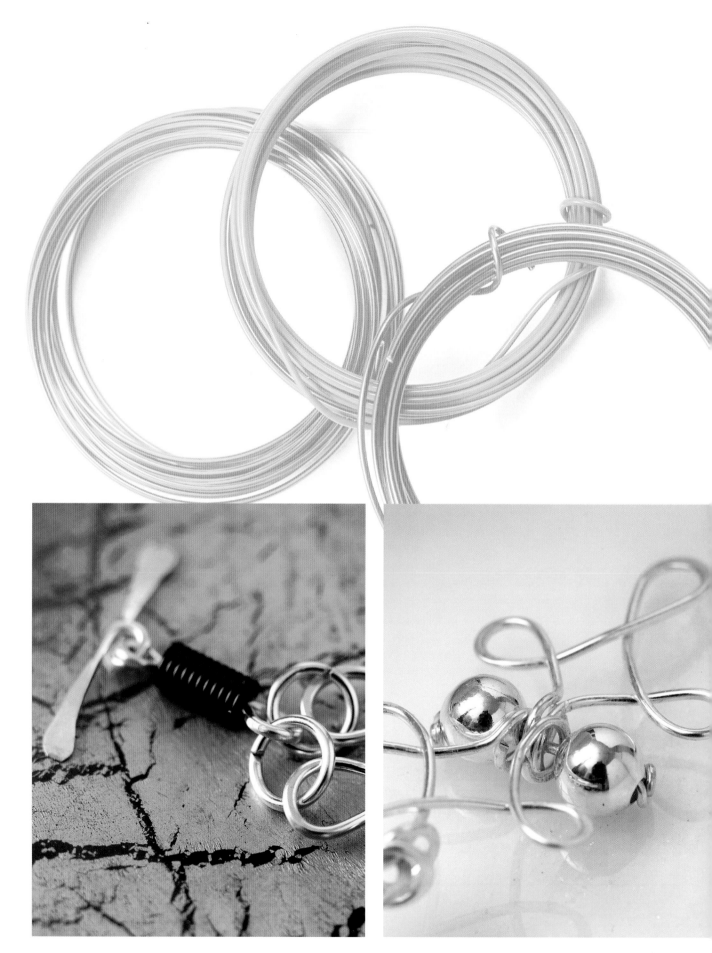

statement chains

Decorative chains lie at the very heart of wire jewelry and the techniques involved in making them, from using a jig to linking elegantly coiled spiral units together, will provide you with a solid base for all your jewelry construction. And don't overlook the potential of using ready-made chains: even lengths of ordinary household plumbing chain can, with a little design flair, be transformed into dramatic pieces of jewelry that belie their humble origins.

magic ladder necklace

This very simple design is made from plumbing chain and looks amazingly effective worn against a plain-colored garment. The single focal bead draws attention to the linearity of the tapered chain "ladder." For more color and a decorative element, thread the horizontal "rungs" of the ladder with beads or charms.

you will need

Approx. 66 in. (165 cm) copper-colored plumbing chain

20-gauge (0.8mm) copper wire

1 x 1-in. (2.5-cm) feature bead

Heavy-duty and standard wire cutters

Round- and flat-nose pliers

1 Using heavy-duty cutters, cut a 15-in. (25-cm) length of plumbing chain. Make a fish-hook clasp and eye (see page 17) from 20-gauge (0.8mm) copper wire and attach to the ends of the chain.

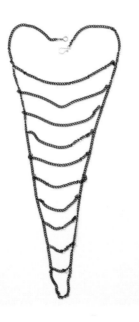

2 Using 20-gauge (0.8mm) copper wire, make 21 jump rings (see page 16). Cut a 24-in. (60-cm) length of plumbing chain. Using jump rings, attach this chain to the first length, with one end 5 in. (12.5 cm) from the fastener and the other end 5 in. (12.5 cm) from the eye. This second length of chain will form the sides of the "ladder."

3 Cut nine more pieces of chain; the first one should be 5 in. (12.5 cm) long, with each of the others ½ in. (1 cm) shorter than the previous one. Using jump rings, attach the cut pieces of chain to the ladder "sides" in descending order of size at 10-link intervals. Cut the base of the ladder frame at the center point, then re-connect the two sides with a jump ring.

4 Thread your chosen bead onto 20-gauge (0.8mm) wire and form a link (see page 12) at each end. Attach the bead to the jump ring at the tip (the narrowest point) of the ladder. Cut a 1-in. (2.5-cm) piece of plumbing chain and connect it directly to the bottom link of the threaded bead, so that it hangs down like a little tail.

hinge-&-bracket
bracket

you will need

20-gauge (0.8mm) wire

8 x 6mm round silver beads

Wire cutters

Round- and flat-nose pliers

Jig and 4 small pegs

Jig pattern on page 126

Hammer and steel stake

This project uses a linking system that is an interesting alternative to jump-ring connections. The jig units are placed together like brackets and connected with threaded beads, providing a hinge that enables the piece to have backward and forward movement.

1 Cut eight 4½-in. (11.5-cm) lengths of 20-gauge (0.8mm) silver wire. Curl one end of each wire into a complete circle and slip it over the first jig peg. Following the pattern on page 126, wrap the rest of the wire around the rest of the pegs to complete the unit. Carefully remove the unit from the jig and "stroke" hammer (see page 20) the outer part of the frame to flatten it.

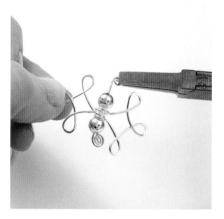

2 Using your flat-nose pliers, twist the first and last loops of each unit through 90°, so that they face each other. Group the units in pairs, back to back, with the turned links facing each other. Gently pull the links on one unit of each pair slightly apart, so that the links of the second unit can lie in between.

3 Cut four 2-in. (5-cm) lengths of 20-gauge (0.8mm) wire. Thread each wire through all the top links on one set of units. Thread a 6mm bead onto each side, then form a small, closed spiral (see page 14), curling the wire right up to the beads. Press the spirals flat against the beads. The wire and beads form a hinge that holds the units together.

4 Make eight jump rings and a fish-hook clasp from 20-gauge (0.8mm) wire (see pages 16 and 17). Connect the hinged units together, using a pair of jump rings between each two hinged units. Finally, use the last two jump rings to attach the clasp to one end of the bracelet.

loop-de-loop lariat

This is a very simple lariat-style necklace. To wear it, simply feed the feature bead through any of the gaps in the chain: gravity will do the rest. This is a great project to make as a gift, as it will fit any size! I used thick wire to thread my chosen beads, as they had large holes; if you use beads with smaller drilled holes, you can use 20-gauge (0.8mm) wire throughout the project.

you will need

16-gauge (1.25mm) and 20-gauge (0.8mm) copper wire

Approx. 5 ft (1.5 m) copper plumbing chain

3 x ½-in. (1-cm) green oval barrel beads

2 x ½-in. (1-cm) blue oval barrel beads

1 x 2-in. (5-cm) rectangular feature bead

Heavy-duty and standard wire cutters

Round- and flat-nose pliers

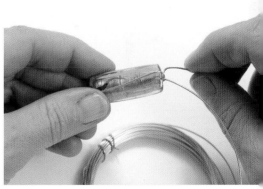

1 Make a jump ring (see page 16) from 20-gauge (0.8mm) copper wire. Open the jump ring, hook it through the last link of one end of the plumbing chain, then hook it through a link 2 in. (5 cm) from the other end of the chain. Close the jump ring.

2 Thread each barrel bead with 16-gauge (1.25mm) copper wire, forming a link (see page 12) at each end. Starting and finishing with a green bead and alternating the colors, attach the threaded beads to each side of the doubled chain at regular intervals. (Count the number of links on each side to make sure that the beads are evenly spaced.)

3 Thread the feature bead onto a spool of 20-gauge (0.8mm) copper wire and pull the wire through and back around to the top bead hole, leaving about 1½ in. (4 cm) projecting. Wrap the projecting wire three or four times around the stem of wire coming from the spool to secure the bead.

4 Cut the wire from the spool, leaving 1 in. (2.5 cm) projecting from the wrapped stem and ½ in. (1 cm) on the end coming from the spool. Form the spool end of the wire into a link (see page 12). At the end of the wrapped stem wire, form a closed spiral (see page 14), then flatten the spiral against the wrapped stem under the link.

5 Attach the feature bead directly to the tail end of the doubled chain. Place your flat-nose pliers vertically on the wire wrapped around the feature bead and twist and tweak to create a wavy pattern and to tighten the wire on the bead.

crossed wires bracelet

This bracelet looks elaborate, but as the units are formed on a jig it is surprisingly simple to make. You could incorporate colored beads within the crossed-wire units, if you wish. I added a touch of color to the clasp to unify it with the jig units.

you will need

25-gauge (0.5mm) colored wire

20-gauge (0.8mm) silver wire

Wire cutters

Round- and flat-nose pliers

Jig and 6 small pegs

Jig pattern on page 126

Hammer and steel stake

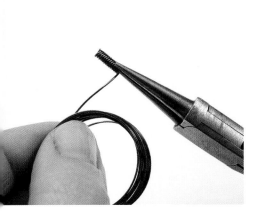

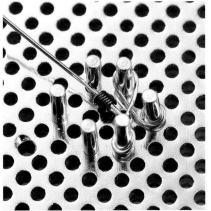

1 Working from a spool of 25-gauge (0.5mm) colored wire, using the tips of your round-nose pliers, form an even, narrow coil about 3½ in. (9 cm) long, in the same way as when making jump rings (see page 16). If you own a Spiral Bead Maker or Coiling Gizmo, use this to make the coil. Cut eight ¼-in. (5-mm) lengths off the coil with wire cutters.

2 Cut eight 5-in. (13-cm) lengths of 20-gauge (0.8mm) silver wire. Form a link (see page 12) at one end of the first wire and slip it over the first peg. Following the jig pattern on page 126, wrap the wire around the pegs in the order shown, threading on a colored coil of wire between pegs 3 and 4.

3 Carefully remove the unit from the jig. Cut off any excess wire and gently "stroke" hammer (see page 20) the outer parts of the unit on a steel stake to flatten and work harden it, being careful not to hammer the colored coils. Repeat Steps 1–3 seven times, to make eight jig units in total.

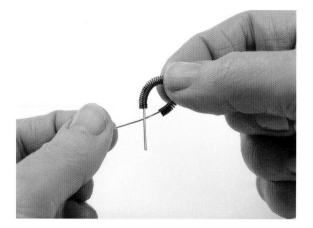

4 Using the tips of your round-nose pliers, carefully uncurl the top and bottom loops on every unit, and form the wires into small, open spirals (see page 14).

5 For the "eye" of the fastener make a wrapped loop (see page 21), shaping the wire around a pencil—but before you secure the wires together, thread on a 1½-in. (4-cm) length of the colored coiled wire that you made in Step 1. Secure by wrapping one wire around the other. Cut off the excess wrapped wire and neaten the end (see page 13), leaving the other wire projecting by about ½ in. (1 cm). Form a link (see page 12) at the end of the projecting wire.

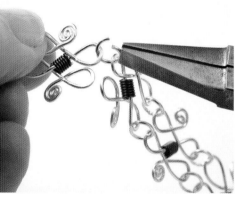

6 Make 17 jump rings from 20-gauge (0.8mm) wire (see page 16). Link the wire units together to form the bracelet.

7 Make a toggle clasp (see page 19), feeding a small coil of colored wire onto the stem before you form the end links. Attach the clasp and eye to the ends of the bracelet via jump rings.

butterfly chain bracelet

The decorative butterfly units on this bracelet can also be made into earrings, used as a pendant on a necklace, or wired onto rings, hair accessories, and even greetings cards. For a more decorative version, use colored wires and thread small seed beads onto the butterfly bodies. The S-link chain units blend in well with the spirals on the butterflies and are useful connectors and linking systems for any jewelry project.

you will need

20-gauge (0.8mm) and 26-gauge (0.4mm) copper wire

20-gauge (0.8mm) brass wire

Wire cutters

Round-, chain-, and flat-nose pliers

Hammer and steel stake

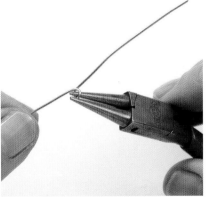

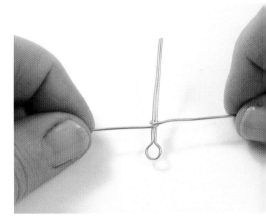

1 For the "body" of the butterfly, cut 3 in. (7.5 cm) of 20-gauge (0.8mm) copper wire. Placing your round-nose pliers in the center, bend the wire in half. Using the tips of your chain-nose pliers, pinch the wires together near the bend to form a loop, with the projecting wires running parallel to each other.

2 For the "wings," cut 4 in. (10 cm) of 20-gauge (0.8mm) copper wire. Fold the wire in half and wrap the center right around the tips of your round-nose pliers to form a loop, with the ends of the wires projecting straight out in opposite directions.

3 Thread the loop of the wings onto the body unit and pull the wires out in opposite directions to tighten them around the doubled wire.

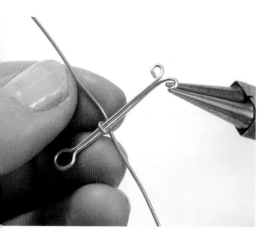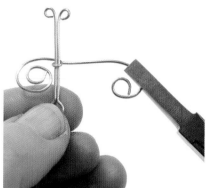

4 Using the tips of your round-nose pliers, make a small link (see page 12) at the end of each of the projecting wires of the body.

5 Form the ends of the wing wires into open spirals (see page 14), curling the wires inward until they touch the vertical wires of the body.

6 Form the vertical body wires into small open spirals, curling them inward on each side until they reach the spiraled "wings," to make tiny antennae.

LEFT *Tiny seed beads threaded onto the butterfly bodies provide a splash of color, while an individual butterfly unit makes a striking yet delicate-looking ring.*

7 "Stroke" hammer (see page 20) the spiraled wings and antennae to flatten and work harden them.

8 Cut about 3 in. (7.5 cm) of 26-gauge (0.4mm) copper wire and wrap it around the doubled-wire stem of the body to secure. Cut off any excess wire and neaten the ends (see page 13). Repeat Steps 1–8 twice, to make three butterfly units in all.

9 Cut three 3-in. (7.5-cm) lengths of 20-gauge (0.8mm) brass wire and make them into spiral S-links (see page 15). "Stroke" hammer (see page 20) the S-links to flatten and work harden them.

10 Make 13 jump rings (see page 16) from 20-gauge (0.8mm) brass wire. Alternating butterfly units and spiral S-links, connect all the units together with jump rings. You need four jump rings for each butterfly unit: one for each spiraled antenna, plus one more to loop through both antennae jump rings, and one at the opposite end.

11 Make a toggle clasp (see page 19) and eye fastener from 20-gauge (0.8mm) brass wire, and attach to the bracelet ends with the remaining jump rings.

LEFT A toggle clasp makes a sturdy yet delicate-looking fastener for this pretty chain bracelet.

notable necklaces

This chapter, perhaps more than any other, shows how simple, inexpensive items—even those not normally associated with fine jewelry, such as flat-backed glass nuggets and a humble household washer—can be transformed into show-stopping conversation pieces. Inspired by the simple design ideas from this chapter, let your imagination run riot and come up with innovative creations of your very own!

memory lane lariat

This design came about when a very good friend of mine turned up with a little box of broken jewelry pieces, following a clear-out of her dressing-table drawer. A broken earring dating back to a holiday in Crete when she was 18; a silver charm that her late father had given her on her 21st birthday; some loose pearls from a broken necklace that had belonged to her grandmother—each piece brought back a cherished memory. I had the idea of creating a "memory lane" lariat for her and I connected all the little pieces like charms, alternating them with her birthstone bead color to unify the necklace.

you will need

20-gauge (0.8mm) silver wire

Selection of beads, charms, drilled coins, or shells of your choice, including a focal bead about 1 in. (2.5 cm) long

Black cotton cord

Wire cutters

Round-, chain-, and flat-nose pliers

Superglue (optional)

1 Pieces that cannot be threaded with wire need a wire "cage" to contain them. Make a spiral S-link (see page 15) from 20-gauge (0.8mm) wire. Bend the unit in half so that the spirals sit on top of each other. Pull out the central circle of each spiral, so that they sit at 90° to the spirals. Holding the circles in your pliers, pull the coils out to make an elongated "cage."

2 Using your fingers, insert your bead and press the wire tightly around it. This cage is for the large focal bead that will go at the end of the lariat; it's about 1 in. (2.5 cm) long, so I used about 7 in. (18 cm) of wire to make the cage.

3 Thread any beads with 20-gauge (0.8mm) wire, forming a link at one end and a head pin at the other (see pages 12 and 13). With drilled "charms" such as coins, hook a jump ring (see page 16) through the hole.

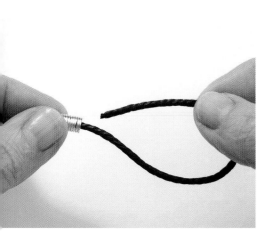

4 Cut a piece of 2mm cord three times the length you want the lariat to be. Make a coil of 20-gauge (0.8mm) wire (see page 16). Slide the coil over the cord, then feed the cord end back into the coil to make a loop. Squeeze the first and last rings of the coil to fasten them onto the cord. Repeat at the other end of the cord.

5 Make the required number of large jump rings (see page 16). Open up each one in turn, hook it into the link on a bead or charm, then close the jump ring. Slide the jump ring onto the cord, then knot the cord over the jump ring to hold each charm or bead in place. Repeat, spacing the beads and charms evenly along the cord.

6 Using a jump ring, connect the focal caged bead onto the loop at the end of the necklace.

vintage button necklace

This decorative necklace is very versatile and can be worn with almost anything, from jeans and a T-shirt to a glam wedding outfit. The sparkle from the three diamanté buttons contrasts with the soft satin finish of the pearls. Look for vintage buttons in thrift stores or flea markets, or ask an elderly relative or friend if they have any that they'd be willing to part with—and if you don't want to use buttons, large beads will do just as well.

you will need

3 x diamanté buttons approx. 20mm in diameter

Assorted round glass pearl beads in browns, mochas, and creams; heart-shaped pearl beads

26-gauge (0.4mm) gold-plated wire

4 x 1mm gilt crimp beads

0.5mm nylon filament

Ready-made clasp

Wire cutters

Round- and chain-nose pliers

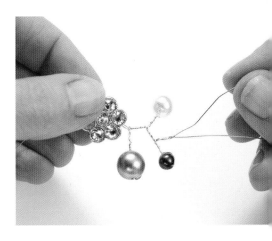

1 Cut six 12-in. (35-cm) lengths of 26-gauge (0.4mm) gold-plated wire. Group the lengths into three pairs. Thread a pair of wires through each diamanté button back. Thread a heart-shaped pearl bead onto the doubled wires on each side, then twist the wires around each other several times to fix the pearl beads in place at the back of the button.

2 Separate the doubled wires out on each side at the back of the button and, leaving a small gap, thread one wire with a pearl bead. Bring the same wire around the top of the bead and bend it back toward the opposite hole. Holding the bead firmly in place, twist the bead three or four times around the second wire to create a twisted stem about ¼ in. (5mm) long.

3 Continue threading and twisting the wires to create beaded branches on each side of the buttons, keeping the design as symmetrical as possible.

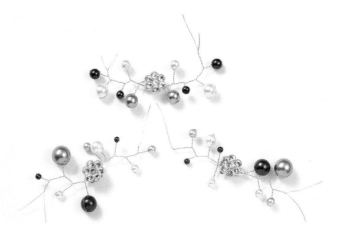

4 Repeat this process, attaching five or six beads to each side of the diamanté button, until you are left with about ½–¾ in. (1.5–2 cm) of wire projecting on at least one of the stems.

5 Once you have threaded all three diamanté buttons in this way, place them together in a row, with the "branches" of the outer units overlapping the center one. Twist the end wires of the two outer units around the center button of the middle unit, making sure they are secured together, then cut off any excess and neaten the ends (see page 13). Twist any overlapping bead stems together to create a solid unit at the front of the necklace.

6 Using the tips of your round-nose pliers, make a small wrapped link (see page 20) at the outer side of each outer unit. Thread each of these links with a length of nylon filament and secure on each side with a crimp bead. The amount of filament you use depends on how long you want to make the necklace; I used about 6 in. (15 cm) on each side.

7 Thread the nylon filament with an assortment of different-sized pearls and secure at each end with a crimp and, finally, a ready-made clasp. Alternatively, make your own fish-hook clasp (see page 17).

ABOVE The same simple technique of twisted-wire "branches" can be used to make matching earrings.

glass nugget necklace

This project demonstrates a simple way of linking together units that do not have drilled holes. I used glass nuggets, which are readily available in both clear and colored versions, but the same method works well with wood, stone, or shells. It is also very important to use a strong glue; E6000 is extremely effective for both glass and metal, and is clear when dry so it will not spoil the appearance of your piece of jewelry.

you will need

20-gauge (0.8mm) silver wire

8 flat-backed glass nuggets, about 1½ in. (4 cm) long

2 x 5mm silver beads

Wire cutters

Round- and flat-nose pliers

E6000 glue

Wooden skewer

1 Cut five 4½-in. (11.5-cm) lengths of 20-gauge (0.8mm) silver wire. Form each one into a spiral S-link (see page 15).

2 Place a small dab of glue on the tip of a wooden skewer and glue each spiral unit to the rounded side of a glass nugget, in the center.

3 Cut sixteen 4-in. (10-cm) lengths of 20-gauge (0.8mm) silver wire. Form each one into a single closed spiral (see page 14), with a link at one end. Using your flat-nose pliers, turn each link so that it sits at 90° to the spiral. Glue one spiral to each side of the back (the flat side) of six of the nuggets, with the links protruding beyond the edge of the nugget.

4 Make jump rings (see page 16) from 20-gauge (0.8mm) wire. Connect the six nuggets from the previous step together in two sets of three (see page 17).

5 Take one of the remaining nuggets and glue two spirals to the top (one on each side) and one to the center bottom, with the links protruding beyond the edge. Using jump rings, attach this nugget between the two sets of three made in the previous step. (This is the first nugget of the center pendant unit.)

6 Glue the remaining spiral to the top of the last nugget, with the link protruding beyond the edge. (This is the second nugget of the center pendant unit.) Cut 2 in. (5 cm) of 20-gauge (0.8mm) wire and thread it through the links of the two pendant nuggets, adding one 5mm silver bead on each side.

7 Form a small, closed spiral (see page 14) on each side of the wire, taking it right up to the beads. Using your flat-nose pliers, flatten the spirals against the side of the beads.

8 For the chain at the back of the necklace, cut six 6-in. (15-cm) lengths of 20-gauge (0.8mm) wire. Form each one into a spiral S-link (see page 15), with a link at each end.

9 Make jump rings from 20-gauge (0.8mm) wire (see page 16). Lay out all the spiral S-links and use the jump rings to join them together in two sets of three. Attach one chain unit made in Step 8 to each side of the necklace. Make a fish-hook clasp (see page 17) and an eye. Attach the clasp and eye to the ends of the spiral-link chain.

LEFT Glass nuggets are available from homeware stores in a range of jewel-bright colors, and make wonderfully shiny and inexpensive "beads." Here, I've put together a random assortment of colors to make a bold, contemporary-looking bracelet.

Glass Nugget Necklace **101**

washer sundial choker

This choker is made by wrapping something as mundane as a steel washer in wire—an inexpensive and imaginative way of creating a necklace that is totally unique! Washers come in varying sizes and, when combined with beaded designs, add weight and give a graphic, contemporary feel to all kinds of jewelry. Once you've mastered the wire wrapping technique, try it out on a semi-precious donut-shaped stone.

you will need

20-gauge (0.8mm) colored wire

Steel washer, 1½ in. (4 cm) in diameter

Shoelace or cotton cord

Wire cutters

Round- and flat-nose pliers

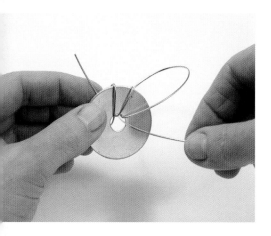

1 Cut about 18 in. (45 cm) of 20-gauge (0.8mm) colored wire. Thread one end through the center hole of the washer, leaving a tail of about 1 in. (2.5 cm) extending. Wrap the rest of the wire around the washer frame, pulling and tightening it with your fingers.

2 Continue wrapping the wire around the washer, leaving even spaces as you go. When you've wrapped the frame about eight or nine times, wrap the working wire around the projecting wire a couple of times, leaving a length extending outward.

3 Form a small, closed spiral (see page 14) with the end of the wire extending from the wrap, curling it in toward the center of the washer. Fold the spiral over and flatten it against the wrapped wire stem with flat-nose pliers.

 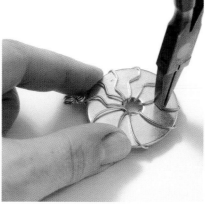 

4 Using your round nose-pliers, curl the remaining projecting wire into a double wrapped link that sits at 90° to the washer.

5 Holding your flat-nose pliers vertically, place the tips directly on each individual wire on the surface of the washer, first on the back and then on the front, and twist to create a zig-zag. This not only tightens the wires around the washer, but also produces a decorative wavy shape.

6 Cut a piece of cord to the desired length and thread it through the top link of the wrapped washer. Make a coiled fish-hook clasp and eye (see page 17) and attach it to the ends of the cord.

LEFT *Matching earrings can be made using different-sized washers and beads.*

chained reaction

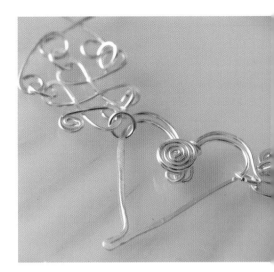

Novice wireworkers sometimes lack the confidence to create freehand wire motifs—it takes a little practise and experience. However, this design has the best of both worlds in that you don't have to worry much about accurate shaping: most of the units are created on a jig and the central heart motif does not have to be regular or symmetrical.

you will need

20-gauge (0.8mm) silver-plated wire

Wire cutters

Jig and 2 small pegs, 2 medium pegs, and 1 large peg

Jig patterns on page 126

Hammer and steel stake

Round- and flat-nose pliers

Cylindrical mandrel, such as a pencil

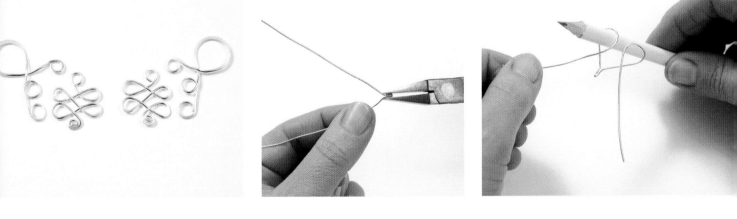

1 Cut two 4½-in. (11.5-cm) lengths of 20-gauge (0.8mm) wire. Following the jig pattern for this project, wrap each one around the pegs. Following the jig pattern for the Crossed Wires project, make two more units, omitting the coiled wire beads and creating a spiral at only one end. Cut off any excess wire and "stroke" hammer (see page 20) each unit.

2 To make the central heart unit, cut 7 in. (18 cm) of 20-gauge (0.8mm) wire. Find the center of the wire and bend it in half, squeezing the doubled ends together with your flat-nose pliers. Straighten the projecting wires out.

3 Place a pencil (or similar cylindrical mandrel) about ½ in. (1 cm) from the doubled end and wrap the wire around it, creating a loop on each wire that curls back in toward the center.

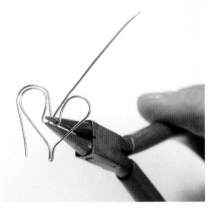

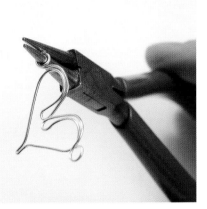

4 Place the tips of your round-nose pliers on the inside of each loop in turn and bend the wire back around with your fingers, following the outer contour you have just created.

5 Using your round-nose pliers, form a link (see page 12) at the end of the wire on each side of the heart frame. Cut off any excess and neaten the ends (see page 13). If you wish, "stroke" hammer (see page 20) the wire frame to work harden and flatten it.

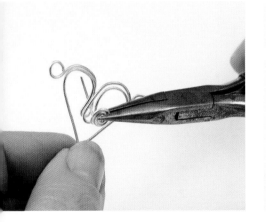

6 Cut 2 in. (5 cm) of 20-gauge (0.8mm) wire. Form one end into a small, closed spiral (see page 14) and thread the unspiraled end of the wire through the center of the heart frame. Form another spiral on the other end of the wire and flatten it against the center to secure it in place.

7 Make 10 jump rings (see page 16) from 20-gauge (0.8mm) wire and connect the two kinds of jig units together in pairs. Make sure the pairs are mirror images of each other.

8 Via jump rings, connect one pair of jig units to either side of the heart shape. (Make sure the pairs are mirror images of each other.) To complete the necklace, connect a handmade S-link chain (see page 15), ready-made chain, ribbon, or cord to each side of the end jig units.

artful adornments

As wire is such a flexible material, there are no bounds to the design combinations that you can fabricate. The accessories in this chapter show how you can create wire frameworks to incorporate "found" objects such as pebbles and feathers in your pieces, alongside traditional beads. All the materials are inexpensive and yet could be created as priceless personal gifts for loved ones and friends.

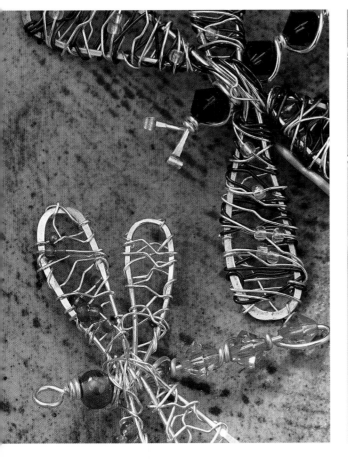

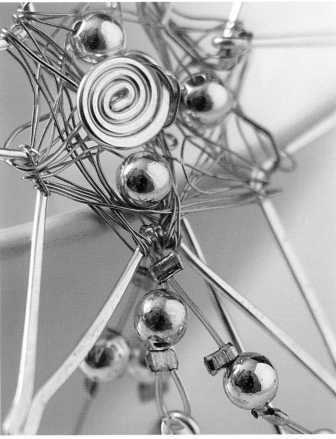

dragonfly hairgrip

If you're looking for a pretty accessory for a little girl, look no further! This simple dragonfly hairgrip will instantly transform her into a party princess. With their gossamer-light wings and iridescent hues, dragonflies provide designers with a wealth of inspiration. Here, I've filled in the wings with a tracery of thin, shocking-pink wire to capture both their delicacy and their vibrancy of color. Enamel-coated wires are readily available in every color of the rainbow—so why not substitute turquoise or sea green for the pink, or perhaps combine blue and purple with a sprinkling of multi-faceted crystals to obtain the ultimate sparkle?

you will need

20-gauge (0.8mm) silver wire
26-gauge (0.4mm) colored and silver wire
5 x 6mm pink faceted crystal beads
Approx. 16 clear and pink seed beads
Hairgrip
Wire cutters
Round- and flat-nose pliers
Hammer and steel stake

1 Cut 7 in. (18 cm) of 20-gauge (0.8mm) silver wire. Bend the wire in two, leaving one end about 2 in. (5 cm) longer than the other.

2 Thread a 6mm bead onto the shorter stem. Wrap the longer wire around the shorter one, above the bead, to keep it in place. Thread a second 6mm bead onto the stem and wrap the wire around, as before.

3 Add two more beads in the same way—but after the fourth bead, wrap the wire twice around the stem to create a slightly bigger gap between the fourth and fifth beads. (More space is needed here as the wings will be secured at this point.)

4 After you have threaded on the fifth bead, wrap and secure the wire above the bead. Pull the projecting wires out into a V-shape (these will be the antennae) and cut them to the same length—about ½ in. (1 cm). Hammer the ends of the antennae on a steel block to flatten and harden them (see page 20), taking care not to hit the beads.

5 Using the tips of your round-nose pliers, curl the ends of each antenna around.

6 Cut 12 in. (30 cm) of 20-gauge (0.8mm) wire. Wrap the center of the wire around the beaded "body," just under the top bead, then straighten out the wires on each side.

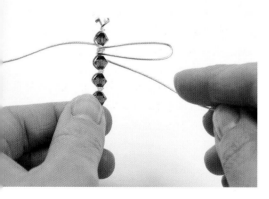

7 Place your round-nose pliers on one projecting wire 1½ in. (4 cm) from the center stem and loop the wire around to create the top wing. Wrap the wire around the center stem to secure, leaving the wire projecting on the other side. Form the second wing in the same way on the opposite side.

8 Using the rest of the projecting wire, form two smaller, lower wings about 1 in. (2.5 cm) in length in the same way, again wrapping and securing the wires just under the top bead. Neaten the ends around the stem (see page 13).

9 Spend a little time adjusting the wings until you are satisfied with their shape. Hammer the ends of the wings to work harden and flatten them (see page 20).

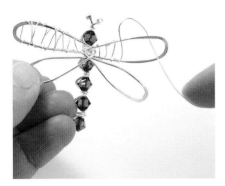

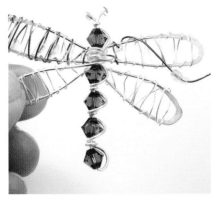

10 Cut 12 in. (30 cm) of 26-gauge (0.4mm) silver wire. Wrap the wire to secure around the "body" stem, just under the top bead. Begin weaving the wire around the frame on both sides, filling up the open areas. Fill in the top wings first, and then the lower ones, cutting a second length of wire for the lower wings.

11 Repeat Step 10, using 26-gauge (0.4mm) colored wire—but this time, add a few clear and pink seed beads for extra sparkle. You can twist and tweak the wires within the wing spaces with the tips of your pliers to add more shape and to toughen the piece.

12 Attach the dragonfly to a ready-made hairgrip by wiring it on with a 3-in. (8-cm) length of 26-gauge (0.4mm) silver wire. Neaten the ends (see page 13) and make sure that no wires are left protruding.

LEFT The dragonfly motif would work equally well as a pendant necklace or wired to a brooch pin. If you want to suspend it from a ribbon or chain as a necklace, make a wrapped link (see page 20) with the wires projecting from the top bead and omit Step 5, as the link will take the place of the antennae.

Dragonfly Hairgrip **113**

hair band
fascinator

Have you ever spent hours searching the stores for a decorative hair accessory for a really special occasion such as a prom, wedding, or dinner gala, only to come home empty handed? Here's a way of creating your own using a ready-made tiara or hair band as a base. You'll definitely be the belle of the ball!

you will need

26-gauge (0.4mm) and 20-gauge (0.8mm) silver wire

Assorted purple, pink, and clear beads, 3–5mm in size

Ready-made metal hair band or tiara

Feather

Button

Wire cutters

Round- and flat-nose pliers

Hammer and steel stake

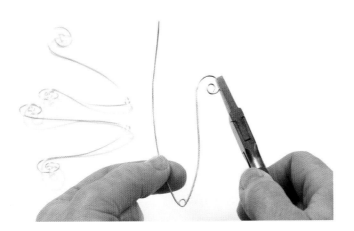

1 Cut one 8-in. (20-cm), one 9-in. (23-cm), and one 10-in. (25-cm) length of 20-gauge (0.8mm) silver wire. Place the tips of your round-nose pliers at the center of each length and curl the wire around into a complete circle (just like the end of a safety pin), with the projecting wires running parallel in the same direction. Form an open spiral (see page 14) at each end of each wire. Hammer the spirals to work harden them (see page 20).

2 Cut about 6 in. (15 cm) of 26-gauge (0.4mm) wire and begin wrapping it around the wires below the spirals, threading on beads as you go. If you run out of wire, cut another length. When the thicker wires are covered with beads, cut off any excess wire and neaten the ends (see page 13).

3 Place the beaded wires together and thread a length of 26-gauge (0.4mm) silver wire through the circular links at the base to join them all, wrapping the wire in and out of the links to secure. Use another length of wire to bind the beaded-wire decoration to the ready-made hair band, positioning it slightly off center, leaving about 2 in. (5 cm) protruding.

4 Thread the projecting wire through the buttonhole from the back, thread on a bead, and then take the wire back through the second buttonhole. Secure the wire at the back by wrapping it around the hair band. Cut off any excess and neaten the end (see page 13). Push a feather into the wired area at the back of the button for extra decoration.

pet stone key ring

I often collect pebbles and stones when I'm on a beach or country walk. This project shows how you can wrap a simple pebble (to keep the memory of a special place or vacation) and turn it into a useful key ring or necklace pendant. This key ring also makes a great gift for a male friend.

you will need

Small stone or pebble

20-gauge (0.8mm) silver wire

Wire cutters

Round- and flat-nose pliers

Ready-made key ring finding

1 Cut a piece of 20-gauge (0.8mm) silver wire about five times the length of the stone and bend it in two. Squeeze the wires together with your flat-nose pliers and straighten them out so that they run parallel to each other. Using the tips of your round-nose pliers, form a circle at the end of the doubled wire.

2 Hold the doubled circle very firmly in your flat-nosed pliers and form a small, closed spiral (see page 14) about ½ in. (1 cm) in diameter. Separate the wires, so that they project at right angles to each other. Place the spiral on the center front of the stone.

3 Bring one wire around the back of the stone from the bottom to the top and the other around the back from side to side.

4 Take the side wire over the front of the stone to the top wire, then wrap it around the top wire to secure. Cut off any excess and neaten the end (see page 13). If you have enough wire left, you can form a small, closed spiral and flatten it against the wrapped wires to hide them.

5 Using your round-nose pliers, form a link (see page 12) with the top wire. Holding your flat-nose pliers vertically, place the tips directly on the wire wrapped around the stone, first on the back and then on the front, and twist to create small zig-zags. This tightens the wires around the stone and produces a decorative wavy shape.

6 Undo the link at the base of your ready-made key ring, hook it through the link at the top of the stone, then close it again to attach the stone to the key ring.

shooting
star pin

This lapel or hat pin has a real Christmassy feel about it, although it can be worn all through the year, bringing a hint of Christmas magic to your everyday life! The "light trails" radiating out from the central star add extra sparkle and movement to the piece—but you could omit these and create a simple star shape brooch, similar to a sheriff's badge.

you will need

20-gauge (0.8mm) silver wire

26-gauge (0.4mm) gold-plated wire

18 x 4mm round silver and gold beads

Lapel pin and protector end

Wire cutters

Round- and flat-nose pliers

Hammer and steel stake

Superglue

0.5mm nylon filament

24 x 1mm silver crimp beads

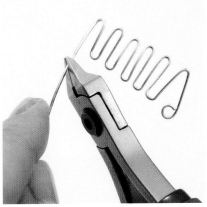

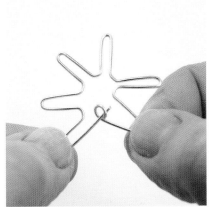

1 Working directly from a spool of 20-gauge (0.8mm) silver wire, use the tips of your round-nose pliers to form a link (see page 12) at the end of the wire. Place the tips of your pliers about ½ in. (1 cm) from this link and bend the wire back toward it, forming a V-shape.

2 Reposition the tips of your pliers level with the link you created in Step 1 and bend the wire back up in the opposite direction. Repeat to create six zig-zags. Cut the wire from the spool, leaving a small tail.

3 Using your fingers, pull each end around to form a circular shape. Using your flat-nose pliers, twist the end link so that it sits at 90° to the zig-zags. Thread the cut end of the wire into this link, and secure by looping the wire around the link. Neaten the ends (see page 13). Adjust the zig-zags with your fingers to make a star.

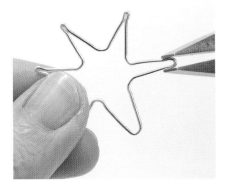 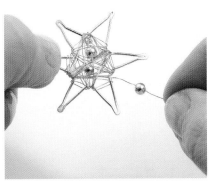 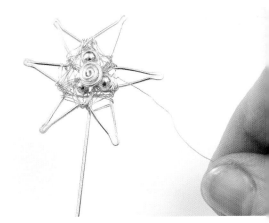

4 Using your flat-nose pliers, squeeze the ends of each zig-zag to form the points of your star. When you are satisfied with the overall shape, hammer the frame on a steel stake to work harden it (see page 20).

5 Cut about 12 in. (30 cm) of 26-gauge (0.4mm) gold-colored wire and wrap it around the center of the star frame in a freeform manner to form a fairly solid mass. Cut another length of wire and attach it in the same way, this time threading on small gold and silver beads as you wrap.

6 Using 20-gauge (0.8mm) silver wire, form a small, closed spiral (see page 14) about ½ in. (1 cm) in diameter. Glue this onto the front of the lapel pin finding. Push the lapel pin through the center of the front of the star, then secure it in place at the back with 28-gauge (0.4mm) gold wire.

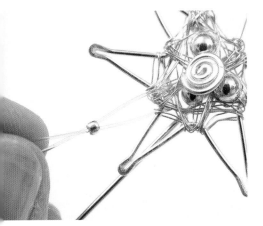 

7 Cut a 4-in. (10-cm) length of nylon filament. Wrap one length around one arm of the star near the pin. Feed a crimp bead onto the filament and press with your pliers to secure. Repeat three times, so that you have four "rays" radiating outward from the base of the star.

8 Thread 4mm round silver and gold beads onto each length of filament in groups of one or two at a time, using a crimp bead at the start and end of each group to secure them in place so that they appear to float off the lines. Cut off any excess filament.

bow brooch

This distinctive brooch looks colorful and feminine, and can be worn on a coat or jacket, secured on a hat, clipped to a bag, or used to fasten a shawl. Part of its charm is that it doesn't have to be symmetrical—so regardless of whether you're a beginner or advanced wireworker, this project will suit all skill levels. I hope it will also inspire you to think of other shapes that you could embellish with colored seed beads in a similar way.

you will need

20-gauge (0.8mm) and 26-gauge (0.4mm) silver wire

Assorted red seed beads

Red button

Brooch back

Wire cutters

Round- and flat-nosed pliers

Hammer and steel stake

Cylindrical mandrel or pencil

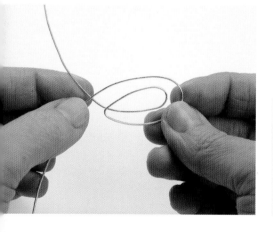

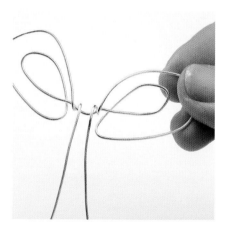

1 Cut 18 in. (45 cm) of 20-gauge (0.8mm) silver wire. Position your pencil (or a cylindrical mandrel) near the center of the wire and wrap the wire around to form a loop. Using your fingers, bring the wire around the first loop to form a larger loop, keeping a space between the two. Don't worry if the shape is irregular—that's part of the brooch's charm.

2 Repeat on the other side of the wire to form the second loop of the bow.

3 Wrap each end of the wire completely around the center point, leaving the loose ends of wire pointing downward. If necessary, adjust the shape of the loops with your fingers.

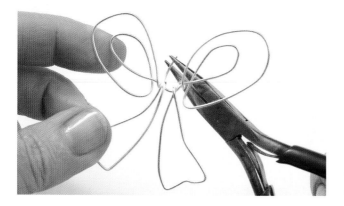

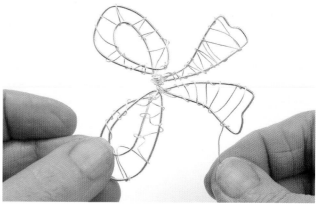

4 Make the ends of the bow by bending each wire in turn into a rough triangular shape with your flat-nose pliers, then secure the ends by wrapping them around the center point, as in the previous step. Spend a little time re-arranging the frame with your fingers, until you are happy with the overall shape. If you wish, gently "stroke" hammer (see page 20) the outer edges of the frame to work harden and flatten it.

5 Cut about 14 in. (35 cm) of 26-gauge (0.4mm) silver wire. Place the center of the wire around the center of the bow and begin wrapping the thin wire around the framework, loosely filling in the space between the two wires of the bow loops. Repeat the process to fill in the "tails" of the bow. Secure the wire ends around the frame, and neaten the ends (see page 13).

6 Repeat Step 5, this time adding colored seed beads as you wrap the wire.

7 Cut 3 in. (8 cm) of 26-gauge (0.4mm) silver wire. Feed it through the shank of the button and bind both ends of the wire securely around the center of the bow. Cut off any excess wire and neaten the ends (see page 13). (If your button has holes rather than a shank, feed the wire up through the bow from the back, through one buttonhole, and then back down through the second buttonhole, and secure on the back.) I also glued a wire spiral to the front of the button for a little extra decoration.

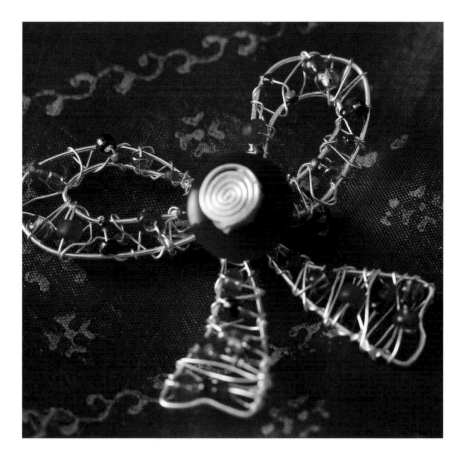

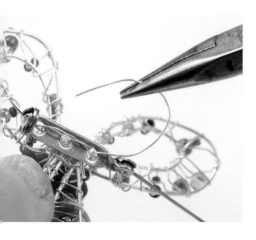

8 Cut 3 in. (8 cm) of 26-gauge (0.4mm) wire. Feed it through the bow brooch and in and out of the holes of a ready-made brooch back to secure it in place.

jig patterns

The patterns shown here are based on a jig in which the holes are arranged in horizontal rows. If your jig has holes arranged on the diagonal, simply rotate it until the holes are aligned as shown below.

Curl the wire around the pegs as shown, following the direction of the arrows.

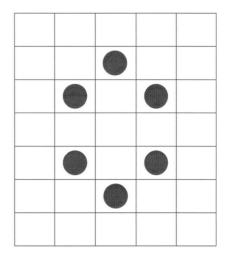

Crossed Wires Bracelet (page 83)

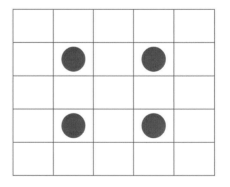

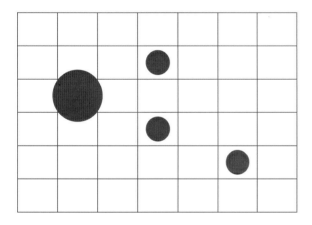

Chained Reaction (page 104)

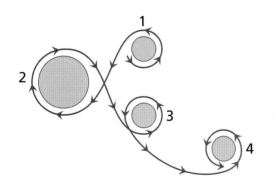

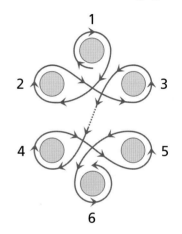

Hinge-and-Bracket bracelet (page 78)

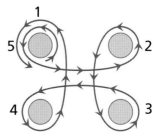

suppliers

UK suppliers

BEADWORKS
21a Tower Street
London WC2H 9NS
Tel. 0207 240 0931
www.beadworks.co.uk

COOKSON PRECIOUS METALS
59–83 Vittoria Street
Birmingham B1 3NZ
Tel. 0845 100 1122
www.cooksongold.com
Suppliers of steel stakes, jewelry tools, and precious metal wires.

CREATIVE BEADCRAFT LTD
1 Marshall Street
London W1F 9BA
Tel. 0207 734 1982
www.creativebeadcraft.co.uk

E-BEADS LTD
Unit TR1-2 Trowbray House
108 Weston Street
London SE1 3QB
Tel. 0207 367 6217
www.e-beads.co.uk

INTERNATIONAL CRAFT
Unit 4 The Empire Centre
Imperial Way
Watford
Hertfordshire WD24 4YH
Tel. 01923 235 336
www.internationalcraft.com

JILLY BEADS LTD
1 Anstable Road
Morecambe
Lancashire LA4 6TG
Tel. 01524 412 728
www.jillybeads.co.uk

MADCOW BEADS
The Bull Pen
Great Larkhill Farm
Long Newnton
Tetbury
Gloucestershire GL8 8SY
Tel. 0844 357 0943
www.madcowbeads.com
Suppliers of Tronex Cutters.

THE SCIENTIFIC WIRE CO.
Unit 3 Zone A
Chelmsford Road Industrial Estate
Great Dunmow
Essex CM6 1HD
Tel. 01371 238013
www.wires.co.uk
(Suppliers of wire only)

WIREJEWELLERY.CO.UK
Faulkners Oast (East)
Tonbridge Road
Hadlow
Kent TN11 0AJ
Tel. 01732 850 727
www.wirejewellery.co.uk
Workshops, DVDs, and expert advice.

US suppliers

FIRE MOUNTAIN GEMS
1 Fire Mountain Way
Grants Pass, OR 97526–2373
Tel: (800) 355 2137
www.firemountaingems.com

JEWELRY SUPPLY
Roseville
CA 95678
Tel: (916) 780 9610
www.jewelrysupply.com

LAND OF ODDS
718 Thompson Lane
Ste 125, Nashville, TN 37204
Tel: (615) 292 0610
www.landofodds.com

MICHAELS
www.michaels.com

MODE INTERNATIONAL INC.
5111–4th Avenue
Brooklyn, NY 11220
Tel: (718) 765 0124
www.modebeads.com

RINGS & THINGS
PO Box 450,
Spokane, WA 99210–0450
Tel: (800) 366 2156
www.rings-things.com

RIO GRANDE
7500 Bluewater Road, NW
Albuquerque, NM 87121
Tel: (800) 545 6566
www.riogrande.com

SHIPWRECK BEADS
8650 Commerce Place Dr. NE
Lacey, WA 98516
Tel: (800) 950 4232
www.shipwreckbeads.com

STORMCLOUD TRADING CO.
725 Snelling Ave. N
St. Paul, MN 55104
Tel: (651) 645 0343
www.beadstorm.com

THUNDERBIRD SUPPLY COMPANY
1907 W. Historic Rte. 66
Gallup, NM 87301
Tel: (800) 545 7968
www.thunderbirdsupply.com

UNICORNE BEADS
404 Evelyn Place, Suite D,
Placentia, CA 92870
Tel: (714) 572 8558
www.unicornebeads.com

WIG JIG
24165 IH-10 West
Suite 217-725
San Antonio, TX 78257-1160
Tel: (800) 579 9473
www.wigjig.com

index

acknowledgments

Thanks to everyone at CICO Books involved in this publication, especially to Cindy Richards for giving me another opportunity to publish my designs. Also my biggest thanks go to Sarah Hoggett, who is without doubt the best editor and adviser I could wish for. Lastly, a big thank you to Geoff Dann, whose photography makes the projects come to life.